TR   ORMING
LEADERS
———— T H E ————
SANDLER
WAY

TRANSFORMING LEADERS
—T H E—
SANDLER WAY

52 Visual Lessons in Personal and
Organizational Effectiveness

DAVE ARCH

Sandler Training

TRANSFORMING LEADERS THE SANDLER WAY
52 Visual Lessons in Personal and Organizational Effectiveness

ISBN: 978-0-9832614-2-1

Visit us at www.sandler.com to learn more!

To my wife, Sue,
who for twenty-five years
has stood as a true partner in life.

Table of Contents

Acknowledgments xi

Foreword... xiii

Read This First

Leadership starts in your own life, and then radiates outward as an example to others.

Transformational Topic:

1. The Big Seven 1

Personal Power

Personal Power is your understanding of the abilities and special skills that have made your past successes possible.

Transformational Topics:

2. Ride the Whole CAB..................................9

3. Positional or Earned? 11

4. Life's Report Card 15

5. Success and Possessions 17

6. The Tombstone Test 19

Conviction

Conviction is your ability to communicate in a positive way about what you think and strongly feel.

Transformational Topics:

7. Passion 23

8. Inner Drive 25

9. Finding Gratitude 29

10. "Never Enough".................................... 33

11. Live Intentionally 35

Charisma

Charisma is your ability to connect effectively, quickly, and deeply with others.

Transformational Topics:

12. Charisma Defined 39
13. The Relationship Pyramid 43
14. Gender Matters 47
15. Personality Matters 51
16. Transactional Matters 57
17. Dysfunctional PAC 59
18. Actions vs. Words 63
19. Networking 65
20. A Lot to Get Past 67

People Skills

People Skills are your ability to "read" people and influence them based on your impressions.

Transformational Topics:

21. Intuitive People Skills 71
22. Wishy-Washy Words 73
23. Top Eight Communication Dysfunctions 75
24. Triangulation 81
25. The Origin of Anger 83
26. Healthy Acceptance 85
27. Boundaries 89
28. Identity vs. Role 93
29. The Mental Credit Card 99
30. Profitability of Pain 101
31. Comfort Zones 103
32. Not Everyone's Cup of Tea 105
33. Anxiety 107
34. Leave Your Child and Your Mother in the Car 109
35. Cognitive vs. Behavioral 111

Courage

Courage is your ability to feel secure in a situation and make others feel secure.

Transformational Topics:

36. The Confidence Paradox 115
37. Social Masks 117
38. Intimidation 119
39. The Reality Room 123
40. Left Brain, Right Brain........................... 127
41. Control 133

Ethics

Ethics is your willingness to act in accordance with clear, consistent principles that connect to a sense of right and wrong.

Transformational Topics:

42. The Principle of the Thing......................... 137
43. Confident Humility 141
44. The OK Test 145
45. You Don't Know! 147

Expertise

Expertise is the practical, specific wisdom that causes others to say, "Wow! I didn't see it that way."

Transformational Topics:

46. Effective Delegation 151
47. Up-Front Contracts 153
48. The Pareto Principle 155
49. Eliminate and Concentrate......................... 157
50. Your Hourly Wage................................. 159
51. The Velvet-Covered Brick 161
52. Epilogue: A Leader's Heart 163

Acknowledgments

I wish to thank the following for their involvement in bringing this project to successful completion. To Dave Mattson, for the opportunity he presented in bringing this book to market through Sandler Training. To Yusuf Toropov, for all his efforts, and for reminding me of a conductor directing an orchestra, making it easy for all the contributing parties to coordinate. To Howard Goldstein, for being the last word. And to Jerry Dorris, for his consistently creative work on the graphics within this book. Thank you to all.

Foreword

Dave Arch's book *Transforming Leaders The Sandler Way* offers a user-friendly, graphically-driven guide to 52 critical leadership lessons that support great careers and great teams. It's required reading for anyone who leads a team or aspires to.

These 52 lessons in personal and team transformation are grounded in Sandler® coaching principles, but they also draw on Dave's ample personal experience as an entrepreneur, coach, and mentor. Those familiar with the core Sandler concepts will find that they serve as the foundation of all that follows. Yet Dave uses these principles to share important new insights about communication, integrity, and personal development.

It's been my privilege to work with Dave, and to see first-hand how he has put these ideas into practical application in his own business. Dave mentioned to me recently that, in one way or another, he's been working on this book for most of his adult life. Reading these pages, I had to agree that his personal experience is what sets it apart from the standard run of "leadership" books. This is something special, and you can prove that in your own world by implementing, and reinforcing, the concepts you will encounter in these pages. Your team and your company will be glad you did, and so will you.

—*Anthony van Dinther, President, Executive Fundamentals, Inc.*

The Big Seven
Leadership starts in your own life,
and then radiates outward as
an example to others.

Read This First:
The Big Seven

Y ou can't transform a team or an organization until you've transformed yourself.

With that idea in mind, I decided to write about the critical leadership principles that support great leaders, great careers and great teams. **Transformational Leadership is leadership that starts in your own life, then radiates outward as an example to others!**

This book is divided into seven sections. Each section reflects a quality I have seen exemplified in the character and work habits of the great leaders I've been privileged to work with over the years. Let's look at each of those seven now.

A leader needs to be someone who has a demonstrated record of **Personal Power.** Now, how you define success is, of course, an individual matter. But if you expect to be followed, you must have achieved a measure of success in some area in which others want to achieve success. Others must be willing to follow you in the hope that you can lead them to similar success in their own world. So: What is your track record? What abilities and special skills made that track record possible?

Conviction means your ability to communicate in a positive way about what you think and strongly feel. Conviction literally means "unshakeable belief." It's what happens when you believe in something so deeply that it actually becomes a part of you. Are you willing to communicate that which is the deepest part of you? Are you eager to do so before anyone else communicates how they feel about the topic under discussion?

Charisma means how effectively, quickly and deeply you connect with others. How easy is it for people to get to know you? Think about figures like Kennedy, Eisenhower and Reagan, whose ability to bond with others quickly was usually more relevant to problem-solving than their politics. Are you, like them, easy to like? Or are you "a lot to get past"?

People Skills means the ability to "read" people and have influence with them. It includes the ability to read subtleties in people's body language. It also includes the ability to learn how to connect with somebody without overlooking the context in which you're communicating. At the end of the day, having people skills means being sensitive to all of the cues that people are sending your way in their communication with you.

Courage is not necessarily about how confident you are as an individual. It has more to do with how secure you make others feel. Does your level of courage cause others to feel secure too? Courage that only causes those around you to remain fearful isn't the kind of courage I'm talking about in this section of the book.

Ethics means that you act in accordance with clear, consistent principles that connect to a sense of right and wrong. You might not know in any given moment exactly what a leader's going to do; but you'll know within what boundaries that leader's going to do it because the leader has clearly communicated the principles and values that guide his or her life.

Expertise is different from what you do. It's what you know. What wisdom and insights do you possess as the result of your personal experience? Expertise is the practical wisdom that causes others to say, "Wow! I didn't see it that way."

These are the seven essential qualities of a leader. They support each other, and no truly great leader is missing any of the qualities.

Each quality operates in an integrated manner with the other six. You can look at the list, mentally remove any one of the points, and instantly understand how deeply any missing element would diminish a leader's strength.

Consequently, each section in this book deals with a single item on the list. *Transforming Leaders the Sandler Way* is based on decades of experience as a Sandler trainer and in other roles, based on work with some of the greatest leaders in American business. It is designed to help you "unpack" each key point and strengthen your own leadership in all seven areas.

This book comes with a companion card deck. In the following card activities, unless otherwise noted, it is assumed that you will only use the cards that correspond with the chapters you have already read and studied.

SOLITAIRE

Challenge yourself to place the cards face down in front you–mixing the cards over the table. Then draw a card at random and see if you can summarize at least three points that support the concept, working only from the prompt on the card. Continue until all the cards are turned over on the table.

FOUR CORNER BATTLE

In this variation for groups, a facilitator instructs teams to gather in four corners of the room where you're playing. (The game works best with between five and seven members per team.) The facilitator distributes the cards evenly to each team and selects one team to begin the game by posing a question. The team must devise a question based on the topic from one of their cards. If the team posing the question does not know the answer without looking into the book, the question cannot be used.

Taking turns, each team selects a question and addresses it to any other team. The responding team gets to conference as a group before answering. The facilitator is the ultimate judge of an answer's correctness. If the responding team answers the question correctly, that team gets to ask one member of the questioning team to sit down. If the responding team doesn't answer correctly, the questioning team must answer the question (correctly!) and may then select one member of the questioned team to sit down. Eventually only one person will be left standing as the winner.

PICK A CARD . . . ANY CARD

In this variation for small groups, the facilitator breaks the group into teams of two. Working in pairs, each pair looks through the deck as a whole and then chooses a card that seems interesting. Each team then goes back to its copy of the book *Transforming Leaders the Sandler Way* to research the principle depicted on the card.

Working together, or with one person doing the talking, each team shares its thirty-second summary with the group as a whole. The facilitator selects a winning team.

Personal Power is your understanding of the abilities and special skills that have made your past successes possible.

TRANSFORMATIONAL TOPICS:

- ☐ Ride the Whole Cab
- ☐ Positional or Earned?
- ☐ Life's Report Card
- ☐ Success and Possessions
- ☐ The Tombstone Test

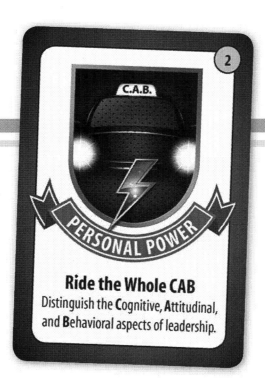

Ride the Whole CAB

ny body of knowledge, including leadership development, has three different but complementary pathways to mastery. There are the Cognitive aspects — the things you need to know in order to be a good leader. There are the Attitudinal aspects — the attitudes you need to carry with you in order to be a good leader. And there are the Behavioral aspects — those things you need to do in order to be a good leader.

This book will be great at giving you the Cognitive aspects.

You will know a lot about leadership when you get done reading it. The Attitudinal and the Behavioral pieces, however, require a different development path in order to be put into place. Meeting regularly with an executive coach can help you to put the attitudinal and the behavioral pieces together. By the same token, meeting with your manager, and meeting with people who can give you feedback on how you're coming across, can also help you to put the attitudinal and behavioral pieces together.

That may include being involved in a 360-peer review, where you get a comprehensive anonymous survey from those people around you. These results tell you not how you want to come across, but how you are coming across. That information has proven itself very powerful in changing attitudes and behavior.

I begin this section with the C-A-B acronym to remind you of the limitations of this book or any book. What you will learn on these pages will fill in the "C" blank, but you still need to call the rest of the "CAB." Here, you will learn what a leader is. You will learn about leadership. But you will not become a leader by only focusing on the Cognitive aspects of this content.

So as we begin, I encourage you to combine the reading of this book with feedback from someone you can trust — a role model, a mentor, someone who will give you honest feedback based on their perception of you. That will help you close the gap on the Attitudinal and the Behavioral components as well.

Positional or Earned?
Build leadership on the personal capital
you've earned, not the title you hold.

Positional or Earned?

974 was a watershed year in the United States. For the first
time, a President resigned from office. Regardless of what
you think of Richard Nixon, or the Watergate scandal, or any
other aspect of the unruly history of that era, there is an important leadership lesson to be learned from what happened in Au-
gust of that fateful year.

Prior to the social revolutions that began playing out in the
1960's, Positional Authority was very much the rule of the land. If

your teacher told your parents that you acted out in school, then, in most cases, you were in trouble. Period. There was no discussion about what happened or didn't happen. There were no conferences in the principal's office. Nine times out of ten, or maybe more, punishment was duly administered. Why? Because the teacher was an authority figure. A Congressman, the President, a parent, a teacher, a boss, indeed any authority figure was respected … due to the position he or she held.

It wasn't just parents. The press respected this, too. We now know that there were many activities going on in President John F. Kennedy's White House that would have generated multiple high-profile scandals in our era. However, not a word of any of them made it into the press. Reporters (and everyone else) protected Kennedy's privacy out of respect for the office of the President.

I'm sure President Nixon thought the rules would be the same for him when he took the oath of office. However, the rules had changed between Presidents Kennedy and Johnson. With the sole exception of the military (and even there, changes are coming), Positional Authority died in the early 1970s.

Nevertheless, Earned Authority is still very much alive. This is authority based on the capital you have built up within the relationship. These days, Earned Authority counts more than Positional Authority. Effective leaders know this. You'll still see "leaders" who don't know any other way to engage their troops without "pulling rank," and telling them what they should be doing without giving them a "why." This is the Nixon approach. It often ends badly.

Usually such an approach produces what might be called a Compliant Child or Rebellious Child response, with the leader never really getting the truth from his or her direct reports.

Management guru Peter Drucker spoke of the skills needed to manage a non-profit organization of volunteers. In such an organization, Drucker observed, one can't pull rank by threatening a pay cut or firing a person! He said that if every leader led the for-profit business as though it were a non-profit, morale would be higher and much greater productivity would result.

Never settle for Positional Authority when the potential for Earned Authority exists!

Life's Report Card
Don't "grade" yourself in
only one area of life.

Life's Report Card

When considering what success means to you, it's important to consider that question in the context of your whole life.

If I came home from school with a report card that had two Ds, two Fs, a C and an A, my parents would not have considered that to be a good report card. Would yours?

I didn't think so. Yet, too many people grade themselves only in one area of life as they seek to determine what success really means.

This card asks you to consider your overall report card in multiple areas of your life. So consider, for instance, the person who receives an A in "Career." That's very successful, right? But look a little further down the report card, and you'll see an F in family, a D in friends, a D in faith, an F in health and a B- in finances.

As you consider what success means to you (and each of us have to provide our own definition), let me challenge you to be sure to consider success benchmarks that address all the important areas of your life – not just one. There are far fewer regrets when "success" is placed in that context.

Success and Possessions
Success is not the same
as owning things.

Success and Possessions

When one begins to pursue success, there's usually a trap waiting to be discovered: Success is not the same as owning or possessing things.

Many people purchase things in order to help them feel successful. If they're wearing the right clothes, driving the right car, living in the right neighborhood, then they feel successful. That's the trap.

There are just never enough things to keep one feeling successful. Some people may even go deeper and deeper and deeper in debt in an effort to satisfy a craving that can only be met on the inside first.

If you only feel successful when you purchase things, you have the cart in front of the proverbial horse. However you choose to define success, you will want to watch out for this trap.

The Tombstone Test
What do you want written
on your tombstone?

The Tombstone Test

This is a simple exercise that can yield profound results. Ask yourself: "What do you want written on your tombstone following your death?"

Your honest answer to that question will bring to the surface those values that are most important to you. Those are the values for which you want to be remembered.

The obvious next question is: "Are you contributing to the epitaph with the choices you make about how you're investing your life today?"

Great leaders do make sure that a focus on what's truly important in their life remains, no matter how busy or preoccupied they may get. They're not frightened of this question. They find within it their desired energy, passion, and drive for accomplishing their daily responsibilities ... with an eye on their ultimate legacy.

Conviction is your ability to communicate in a positive way about what you think and strongly feel.

TRANSFORMATIONAL TOPICS:

- ☐ Passion
- ☐ Inner Drive
- ☐ Finding Gratitude
- ☐ "Never Enough"

Passion
Connect with people on the
level of thoughts and feelings.

Passion

Just about everyone agrees that passion is an indispensable
component of good leadership. But what *is* passion? Why is
it so powerful?

People communicate on many different levels and convey
many different messages: pleasantries, clichés, facts about others,
facts about yourself, your thoughts and your feelings. The deepest
part from which we share is our thoughts and our feelings.

I can talk in pleasantries and clichés and not make myself vulnerable to anyone. For instance, if a baseball team that you and I both like is in the World Series, I can mention that, and you and I can have a conversation about it. I can tell you facts about others and not be vulnerable. I can even tell you facts about myself and not necessarily be vulnerable. However, when I start sharing with you my most important thoughts and my feelings, I open myself up to your judgment ... and I do become vulnerable.

When two people connect authentically on the level of thoughts and feelings, they have connected on the deepest level. And that's what passion is all about. Passion says, "I don't care what anyone says about this. This is who I am. I believe strongly that so-and-so needs to happen." Passion declares one's thoughts and feelings unilaterally – disregarding in the moment how others might feel about them. It takes a certain amount of trust in someone else to share that — in any relationship. Once you do share it, people know exactly where you stand.

Without any analysis, others who see passion from you understand that you are being openly, consciously vulnerable about what you believe without care for your own safety. You are stating just how strongly you feel about something, just how important it is to you that something happens (or not happens). You are going out on a limb.

That takes personal strength, and personal strength is what gives passion so much power. It takes strength to be passionate, to be enthused, and go after something, to unilaterally declare your thoughts and feelings. That's why there aren't many who do it ... and why passion is one of the indispensable components of being a good leader.

Inner Drive
Tap into sources
of internal energy.

Inner Drive

No doubt you've seen people who always seemed to need some kind of external motivation to get things done. If someone wasn't standing over them with a stick, they just didn't do anything. And I bet you've seen others who get up early and stay up late, who pursue their dreams day after day after day, and continue to work as though propelled from some inner force.

There are four sources of internal energy that require no external stimulus whatsoever. Take a look at the following graphic:

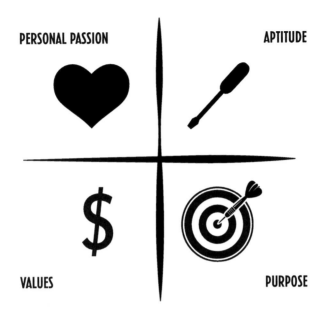

PERSONAL PASSION	APTITUDE
VALUES	PURPOSE

Let's begin in the upper left-hand corner, Personal Passion. When you find out what you love to do, what excites you most about life, the child inside of you who says, "I really enjoy doing this!" So: What do you want to do, love to do, believe in doing? The answer to that is an internal form of energy.

Next, in the upper right-hand quadrant is Aptitude. When you're doing something you're good at, that can be energizing. This has its limits, of course — you can be very good at typing and not feel energized while you're doing it — but you see what I'm getting at. Mastery in a given area often carries its own internal energy.

Then there is the lower left-hand quadrant: Values. When you're doing something that supports your values, you find satisfaction and motivation.

The lower right-hand quadrant, Purpose, may sound a little more nebulous, but it's just as important. All the truly successful people I have ever met had an indescribable sense of purpose, of destiny, of "This is what I was made to do." They have this internal compass that points them toward what they were created to do, what is a perfect fit for them.

Sometimes this purposeful internal energy comes from looking at the unique circumstances in their lives and what they were given: What experiences they were given that others weren't, what hardships they overcame, what they were uniquely prepared to do.

If you have all four of these dynamics going for you, then you have internal motivation, which is a universally admired trait among great leaders. Whenever a person is able to bring together personal passion with aptitude, with values, with a true sense of purpose – that person has found the bull's eye. No one has to get that individual out of bed in the morning.

Internally motivated people go after what they really want — not because someone else told them to, but because they've found their own four internal sources of energy.

CONVICTION

Finding Gratitude
Authentic gratitude motivates
and inspires others.

Finding Gratitude

Aspirit of gratitude has to be one of the strongest internal sources of energy upon which any leader can draw. I've seen this truth firsthand. I've seen it in Togo, West Africa, where highly motivated leaders propel themselves forward with a spirit of deep gratefulness for what little they have. And I've also seen the other side of the coin, where some leaders I've worked with have lost altitude because they couldn't manage to find gratitude in the midst of all they'd been given.

This card seeks to help us identify the components that either deliver gratitude ... or sap our lives of this life-giving force.

Gratitude is found in the comparison of what you believe you deserve with what you've been given (or not given). By "not given" I'm not speaking about a Porsche, a large home, or lots of money. I'm speaking about the fact that you weren't given, say, leukemia, cancer, or children with those conditions (assuming that to be true, for sake of the example).

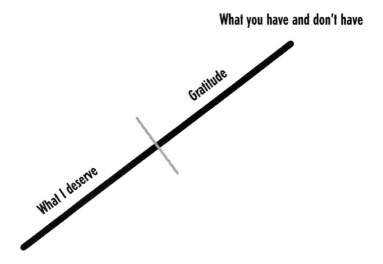

What you have and don't have

Gratitude

What I deserve

Look at the bottom half of the line above and you'll see the words "What I deserve." We all have to fill in that blank for ourselves. What do you feel you deserve in life? What does life owe you?

As the hash mark on the line moves lower (i.e., as you feel you deserve less), the greater your capacity for gratitude (shown on the top half of the line) will be.

So . . . if gratitude is lacking in your life . . . check yourself on what you believe you deserve. It might need adjusting. Then check your "grateful list" to make sure it includes those things that have NOT happened to you, as well as those which have.

Making changes in either or both directions helps great leaders find the gratefulness they need to inspire and motivate others. What can you be grateful for right now?

"Never Enough"
True leaders do not brood on difficult events.

"Never Enough"

I f you've ever known someone who just couldn't seem to find the deep, productive energy that comes from gratefulness, you will want to consider this card closely!

Think of someone you know who encountered some event (or events) that he or she deemed so "unfair," that no matter how many good events were added to the other plate of the scale, they could never balance out the difficult experiences. Nothing is ever enough.

True leaders do not brood on difficult events.

Don't be a "never enough" person – and when you run into such people, see if you can help them to change the way they look at the world! The following quote from author Melody Beattie is a good place to start.

> *"Gratitude unlocks the fullness of life. It turns what we have into enough, and more. It turns denial into acceptance, chaos to order, confusion to clarity. It can turn a meal into a feast, a house into a home, a stranger into a friend."*
>
> — **MELODY BEATTIE**

Live Intentionally
Have goals, plans, and
the vitality to pull the trigger.

Live Intentionally

A great leader lives and leads intentionally. Many others simply allow life to happen to them. A great leader, on the other hand, has goals and plans and the vitality to pull the trigger on those goals and plans. This creates energy, enthusiasm, and passion.

I run into plenty of so-called "leaders" who are merely living life aimlessly. They imagine they are helping others reach their goals and plans without any defined goals and plans of their own.

In fact, they are usually more of a hindrance than a help to the people they "lead."

When I use the two words Live Intentionally in my executive coaching sessions, no person has ever failed to understand what I meant. Do you desire such a life? You already know the answer. To a true leader, intentional living isn't an option . . . it's a necessity.

Charisma is your ability to connect effectively, quickly, and deeply with others.

TRANSFORMATIONAL TOPICS:

- ☐ Charisma Defined
- ☐ The Relationship Pyramid
- ☐ Gender Matters
- ☐ Personality Matters
- ☐ Transactional Matters
- ☐ Dysfunctional PAC
- ☐ Actions vs. Words
- ☐ Networking
- ☐ A Lot to Get Past

Charisma Defined
Are you moving the
relationship forward?

Charisma Defined

Certainly, in a leader's skill set, Charisma is an indispensable component. Most people don't grasp, however, that Charisma has to do with what you choose to communicate about, and when.

As you can see on the triangle, Cliché is the shallowest of the levels of communication. This level of communication is also known as the Pleasantry. (i.e., "Hey how's it going?" "Hey what's happening? Isn't the weather great?" "Absolutely!")

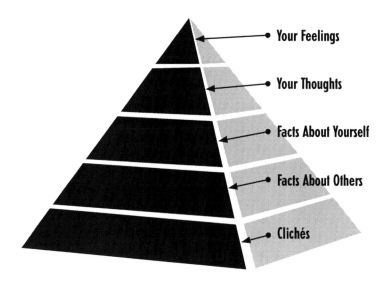

Facts About Others might include "Did you hear what happened to —," "Did you know that so-and-so went on a trip to —".

Facts About Yourself become more personal (i.e., "I was born in Ohio," "I had a family of five," "You know, my dad worked at the coal mine.")

Facts About Your Thoughts And Feelings sound like this: "Here's what I think about that ..." "Here's how I feel about that ..."

People beginning a relationship typically begin at the cliché level. That's the safest level.

Obviously, if a man passes a lady in the hall and says to her, "How's it going?" and she ignores him, that's probably where the relationship is going to stop. Either party can stop the movement towards the middle level, the level of facts about others and facts about oneself, at any time. It takes two to move towards the middle.

But let's say the lady says, "Fine! How's it going with you?" And he says "Fine." And they both smile. Then the next time they see each other, it's in the break room and they pass and they say, "Hey did you hear that ..." and they talk about something that they'd both heard about some celebrity or politician.

Pretty soon they're saying, "Are you from around here?" And then the next thing you know they're each talking about where they were born.

If both are in agreement about forward motion in the relationship, they continue to move up that pyramid until – guess what? They're talking about their thoughts, they're talking about their feelings, and they've reached that deepest part of revealing/sharing themselves.

That's where they're going to be most vulnerable because that's where the opportunity for rejection is the highest!

Leaders who understand this progression work through the steps of this Charisma Pyramid effortlessly, and many have an unconscious competence about it. However, if you do not connect easily with people, you'll want to know how it works so that you can at least begin to work this process by rote.

What happens if you don't follow this sequence? What happens if you either don't stop when the other person indicates "Stop," or you reveal too much too quickly? You kill the potential for Charisma.

Have you ever seen someone jump over some of these stages, getting right to the thoughts, right to the feelings, before establishing connection with a cliché, and before talking about others? What happened? My bet is that you responded, either quietly or out loud, with some variation of "TMI" (Too Much Information).

There's a pattern to the process, an ebb, a flow. There's a gradual coming together. That's Charisma. Without it, you may find yourself putting 90% of the work into the relationship and the other person puts in only 10%. Surely, we've all been in relationships where you wondered if they'd ever call you if you didn't call them. That's not a place we want to be.

Charisma means you know how to work the Pyramid to connect with another person effortlessly, smoothly and seamlessly—allowing them choices in their ability to connect. And that's the key. You can't force this.

I might want to be a trusted advisor to a customer or client, but if that person doesn't want me to be a trusted advisor, I won't be one, because they will stop me. They will hold me back from getting to my thoughts and my feelings, because they won't have responded reciprocally in the preceeding stages.

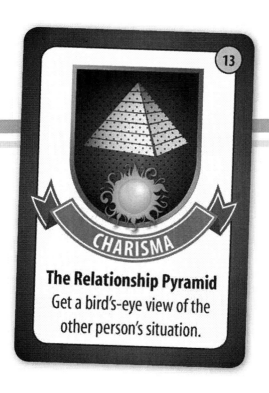

13

CHARISMA

The Relationship Pyramid
Get a bird's-eye view of the
other person's situation.

The Relationship Pyramid

A mentor of mine by the name of Al VerBerg wrote this model out on a napkin for me in the early 1970s. Before he did, he said that in all of his years as a counselor, he had never found anything that described a strong relationship better than this pyramid. He had been in a counseling practice for over 30 years!

Al drew a pyramid with the word "Happiness" at the top. He

said, "Nobody gets married believing that their life is as happy as it could be, with the goal of 'Let's see if we can't make it more hideous by getting married.'"

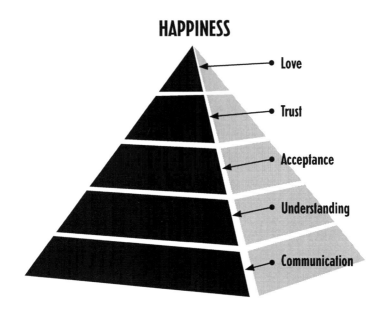

HAPPINESS

- Love
- Trust
- Acceptance
- Understanding
- Communication

Al was right. We enter into relationships in order to increase our happiness. But what is happiness? You've certainly seen couples who have made you wonder, "Why isn't he happy with her?" Or vice versa: "Why isn't she happy with him?"

At the root of happiness, Al taught me, is our own expectations. Possibly, the husband's expectations are so high that he'll never be happy. Or the wife's expectations are so low that she can be happy with him.

Al showed me how expectations are built in relationships from the bottom up.

Communication. Very often, two people only communicate when they have something to discuss that's a crisis. Effective communication, however, requires far more than that. There are many levels of communication — the Cliché/Pleasantry level, the Facts About Others level, the Facts About Yourself level ... but sharing your thoughts and your feelings is the deepest level of all.

Strong communication in relationships is what happens when I talk about and share my thoughts and my feelings with you so you can come to look at the world through my eyes, and vice versa. You'll begin seeing what I see so that I start to make sense to you, and you can grow to an understanding of me.

When I used to do marriage counseling, in the first meeting I would oftentimes ask the man to sit in one corner of the room and the woman to often sit in another, and tell them to write lists. I said, "Complete this sentence: 'For the life of me, I can't understand why he...' Or: 'For the life of me, I can't understand why she...'" So he would complete that list. And she would complete the list. Whenever I saw that they each turned that sheet of paper over, and were still writing, I knew we had a lot of work to do! Their list of what they didn't understand about each other had grown quite lengthy, indicating that there had not been meaningful communication (which is the sharing of thoughts and feelings). When two people share thoughts and feelings authentically, they each understand where the other person is coming from. Minor annoyances are easier to overlook.

Imagine for a moment that you return to the office after a morning meeting, and you greet the receptionist by saying, "What a beautiful day!" And the receptionist says in response: "Oh, shut up!"

You're kind of taken aback. You return to your desk, and you start thinking about that response. You stew a little bit, and you start getting angrier and angrier.

Finally, you go to lunch (obviously not with the receptionist). It's during lunch that someone says, "Did you hear what happened to so-and-so?" and mentions the receptionist's name.

You lean into the conversation only to hear the other person say, "Her husband asked her for a divorce last night."

What happens next? Well, I hope you return to the office changed. The receptionist didn't change. She's just as surly as the last time you saw her, but it no longer bothers you because you've added some understanding to the picture. In fact, you've added acceptance of where that person is coming from because you've received that piece of understanding.

Very often we find that somewhere along the line, we may have picked up the thought that "I can hate things out of my life." For instance: If I just hate myself being fat, I'd get skinnier. If I just hate myself being unkind, I'm going to become kinder. But experience shows us that trying to hate things out of our lives only drives them in deeper.

Al taught me that changing expectations starts with making the effort to get a bird's-eye view of the other person's situation, so we can really understand what's going on, as opposed to trying to hate it out of existence.

Trying to hate things out of another person's life has the exact same result as trying to hate it out of your life. It only drives the problem deeper. It is only within the realm of acceptance that we find ourselves changing and not digging in our feet.

Only as we grow in that acceptance can we ultimately build some trust into the exchange. Then even in business relationships we can grow to where we love the people with whom we work. Yes. You read right. The word I used was "love." I mean caring about them and their well-being that deeply.

Leaders who grow to the place where they care that deeply about his or her followers will have followers who will go the distance for them. However, as Al's Relationship Pyramid reminds us, such relationships must be built one step at a time!

Gender Matters
Surprise, surprise: Men and women
view situations differently.

Gender Matters

L ooking for a reliable recipe for stress? Try to make one gender behave and respond like the other, and then get frustrated
because they "just aren't the same." You'll work yourself into a
stressed condition every time.

There are big differences between the genders in terms of how we
see things and how we think. Gender really does matter. To the ex-
tent that we can embrace the truth of this, it's going to help us greatly
benefit from what each gender contributes to a given situation.

Let's start by considering how men are likely to look at workplace situations (or any other situations).

In the past few decades, we've been able to learn a lot about this as a result of brain scans created with magnetic resonance imaging (MRI) systems. We've been able to understand that men's and women's brains really are "wired" differently.

Women have many more connectors between the left and the right side of their brain. Many more connectors mean they can fluidly go back and forth between the left side (which is the logical side) and the right side (which is the emotional side). The female can just pass back and forth. Ask a female colleague "How do you feel about so-and-so?" and you are likely to hear something like: "I feel like this...." Ask her, "What do you think about this?" and you are likely to hear, "I think ...." I'm generalizing, of course, and no, I'm not a brain scientist, but I think if you look at your own experience, you will see that women are, as a general rule, more comfortable going back and forth between the emotional realm and the logical realm.

When you say to a male colleague, "How do you feel about so-and-so?" though, I'll bet you can almost hear the grinding of the gears. He doesn't have as many connectors between his left and right brain. He's going to get over there in a minute and he'll be able to tell you how he feels, if you give him adequate time. It just doesn't happen fluidly.

You can think of a man's brain as being divided into boxes. You can think of a woman's brain as a system in which information is much more likely to be perceived as interconnected.

Consequently, when they each look at the same situation, the man thinks he's seeing the whole situation. For him it's like looking at life through a telescope. He holds that telescope up to his eye, and he looks down at what he sees through the lens, and he says, "Okay, I see it!"

And yes, he does. He sees "it". He thinks he sees everything, because he sees everything that he sees, but he doesn't see the broader picture. A woman thinks in terms of connectedness, not compartmentalization, and so she is more likely to see the situation as it relates to other components of the situation with a much broader view.

This is particularly true in my house as I stand in front of the refrigerator and I say, "Where's the ketchup?" I can't see the ketchup. I don't know if any of the women reading this have ever had the experience of someone in their life not seeing the ketchup, but my wife certainly has.

It's overwhelming the number of things that are in there. Eventually, my wife comes in and hands me the ketchup, which was right there in the door all the time. It was right there. I couldn't see it. I was overwhelmed by how much there was to choose from.

By the way, I want to give a special thanks to the video series by Mark Gungor entitled *Laugh Your Way to a Better Marriage* for awakening me to the differences that follow. Search for snippets of it online. I found him on YouTube and ordered his DVDs very quickly.

Due to the little boxes/compartments that are in the brain of the man, when a female says to a male, "Let's talk about the kids," he probably goes into his brain and he pulls down the "kid box."

He lifts the lid on the kid box and looks down into the box–beginning to talk about the kids. When he's done, he puts the lid back on the box, he takes the box, he lifts it up, and he slips it back into its slot on the shelves.

The woman taking part in this discussion is likely to approach it very differently. The kids are connected to the mom, the mom's connected to the dad, the dad's connected to the in-laws — it's all connected. It's not in neat little compartments.

Guess what else? There's another gender aspect that occurs when one or the other is under stress. When a man experiences stress and tries to decompress from the events of the day, he typically "zones out" and lets his mind go blank – thinking about literally nothing. He's fine with nothing for a while!

When a woman is stressed, she wants to *talk through* her stress. This is a significant difference that women often have a challenging time understanding.

She'll look at her man and say, "What are you thinking about?" and he'll say, "Nothing." She'll say, "That can't be."

It can be. A man's brain is able to go into neutral and think about nothing. That's how he decompresses, that's how he gets the pressure off. That's how he relaxes.

She'll say, "Do you want to talk about it?" and he'll say, "No." "You've got to be thinking of something. Are you keeping something from me?" "No." And he's not, but it doesn't seem that way to her because she has no comparable process. It can make her crazy, but these are the realities of the genders.

Together, with their unique approaches celebrated and utilized to the fullest, the genders are an unbeatable team. No great leader I have ever met got to be great by fighting the reality of these two different, gender-based thinking dynamics.

We have a saying around my office: "Reality will win."

Here's the point. The woman who sees this overwhelming amount of information as she looks at a situation is helped by the man who's able to bring focus; and the man who could maybe only see just a part of the big piece is helped by the woman as she brings the context of that piece on which he's focused. Not only that, she may bring the context of all the other pieces that might be touching that piece!

Personality Matters
Dominant? Influencer?
Steady Relator? Compliant?

Personality Matters

L et's look at four different ways people choose to be in the world — that is, four ways they've chosen to keep themselves feeling secure.

One group of people went over to a window, looked out the window at the world and said, "It's cruel and unpredictable out there. I want to figure out how to go out there and not be hurt." They decided that people don't get hurt if they stay in control. They decided they were going to be in control of all facets of their lives. That way, they'd only have themselves to blame if anything went wrong. They became **Dominant.** These are the people who take charge. They're in control. They're not afraid of risk. They're not afraid of win-lose challenges. They get things done. **If you want to compliment a Dominant, you would say, "You sure get a lot done."**

Another group of people went over to the same window asking the same question: "How can I keep myself from being hurt out in a world that looks unpredictable?" They came away with a very different answer. They said, "I see what gets people hurt. It's when other people don't like you. I am going to remain likeable." These are our **Influencers.** If Dominants are our task people, Influencers are our "people" people. Influencers are the gregarious ones in the room. They get energy from social situations. **If you want to compliment an Influencer, you would say, "I really enjoy working with you."**

By the way, if you were to say, "You sure get a lot done!" to an Influencer, the person might think, "Yep, all they care about is my productivity." If you say to a Dominant, "I sure enjoy working with you," the person wouldn't necessarily even know what you meant.

There's a third group of people who went over to the window and looked out. These folks said, "No, no, no. The first two groups each have it wrong. It isn't about being in control. It isn't about being liked. It's moving too fast that gets you hurt. It's not processing thoroughly. That's what gets people in trouble: Exceeding the speed limit. Not me, though!" These people became what we call the **Steady Relators** in life. These are the people who live to put one foot very slowly in front of the other. They have to process things thoroughly. Can you guess what their favorite Aesop's fable is? Right! They love the story that reminds everyone that it's not the hare that wins the race; it's the tortoise that wins the race. "Slow and steady wins the race" is the mantra of Steady Relators. **If you want to compliment a Steady Relator, say, "You sure put a lot of time and attention into so-and-so."**

A fourth group of people went over to that same window and looked out, and by now you've guessed that they had a different take on things. They looked out the window and said, "No, no, no. The three of you have it wrong. It's not being in control, as the Dominants have said. It's not being liked, as the Influencers have said. It's not being slow and steady, as the Steady Relators said. It's attention to detail!" For these folks, "The devil is in the details." These are the **Compliants.** For them, compliance with standards is what really matters most. They double-check everything and look around every corner three times. If you're making a presentation, they are the ones who will ask you questions about details you never thought about — unless, of course, you are a Compliant too, in which case you are likely to find yourself in a detail-noticing contest!

Now, at this point, you are probably finding yourself in strong agreement with one of these groups. That's a good thing to notice ... and a potentially dangerous place to be. Let me show you why.

Take a moment and cross your arms in front of you. Don't think about whether it makes sense to do what I just told you to do. Don't worry about whether or not anyone is watching. Just cross your arms in front of you. Did you do that? Good.

Now whether your left hand went over your right arm, or whether your right arm went over your left arm, was solely a matter of habit. Now, though, I want you to reverse arms.

Uncomfortable, right?

Here's my point. You couldn't say it was "right" or "wrong" to have the left arm over the right arm, or the right arm over the left arm. It has become a matter of personal choice and comfort. And so it is with Dominants, Influencers, Steady Relators, and Compliants. They have decided on a certain way they want to be in the world.

DIRECT and CLOSED (likely DOMINANT)	**DIRECT and OPEN** (likely INFLUENCER)
INDIRECT and CLOSED (likely COMPLIANT)	**INDIRECT and OPEN** (likely STEADY RELATOR)

Let's dig into this a little deeper. Notice that people find their comfort zone on a line between Direct and Indirect. That's the vertical line you see here. As a meeting begins some people want to be right up in your face. "So, tell me, why are you here?" Other people will say, "Well, it sure is a nice day, isn't it?" then come to the topic indirectly. There are people all along that continuum in terms of their personal comfort zone.

By the same token, some people are Open, while others are Closed. That's the horizontal axis. Open people usually say, "Ask me what you want to know. I'll tell you." Closed people say, "How am I? Why do you want to know?" Everybody is somewhere on that continuum.

Direct and Closed people tend to be Dominants. Direct and Open people tend to be Influencers. Open and Indirect people tend to be Steady Relators. Closed and Indirect people tend to be Compliants.

What does all this mean? Consider: In order to build Charisma (which is the ability to relate to a wide variety of people), you need to become increasingly adept as a leader in assuming the characteristics of the particular person to whom you want to relate ... not just the people who agreed with you when you looked out the window. In other words, you have to adapt. This is something great leaders learn to do.

If you want to relate to a Dominant type, you'll pick up the pace. If you want to relate to an Influencer, you'll remain in social conversation (some might even call it chit-chat) longer. If you want to relate to a Steady Relator, you will honor their desire to process things thoroughly. You will not push them. If you want to relate to a Compliant, you will give them all the details they need to make a decision, even though you might not be a detailed person.

I have found that the single greatest consideration for matching another person is that of matching their rate and volume of speech. It has been my experience that more than any one component, matching people in their pattern of speech will tend to put you in a position for matching the way in which they wish you to relate to them.

DISC, a system developed by Walter Vernon Clarke, is a wonderful model for understanding the way people are comfortable being in the world. It can help you learn to relate to others in a manner that keeps them comfortable without throwing them into insecurity. As we know from experience, when any of us becomes insecure, it isn't pretty.

Transactional Matters
We talk to each other from one of three
ego states: Parent, Adult, or Child.

Transactional Matters

Sometimes referred to as "Transactional Analysis" or TA, the "Parent-Adult-Child" model gives us a good starting place for understanding interactions with others and building our charisma as leaders. This model suggests that we talk to each other (that is, engage in transactions) from one of three ego states.

For instance: I can speak to you from my Parent Ego State, my Adult Ego State, or my Child Ego State.

Actually, I have three children: I have a Rebellious Child, a Compliant Child and a Natural Child.

A Rebellious Child lives just below the surface. It's the part of me that just wants to scream, "You're not the boss of me."

So when you come at me with your Critical Parent, you run the risk of tripping my Rebellious Child ... or perhaps you'll summon my Compliant Child. My Compliant Child is that part that wants to please. I might tell you what I think you want to hear, but the odds are good that I am not really telling you the whole truth.

My Natural Child is that playful part of me. I bet you know who that kid is, too. Woo hoo!

The Child Ego State never gets emotionally older than seven years old. That part of us has all the fears, concerns, and self-discipline of a seven year old.

The Adult Ego State has no emotion. All emotions reside within the Parent and the Child Ego State. The Adult would say, "That could be a problem" with no emotion (not even a raised eyebrow).

In relating to others as the most effective leaders do, I find that the ideal is to relate 70% from your Nurturing Parent, and 30% from your Adult. Don't let the Critical Parent speak, and don't let the Rebellious, Compliant, or Natural Child in the room. We say, "Leave the Child in the car."

When tempted to go to your Critical Parent, go to your Adult. This takes practice! Just remember the example I gave you. The Adult would say, "That could be a problem" with no emotion either verbally or non-verbally in the expression of the words. By taking that approach, you do not trip an emotional reaction in the other person. Instead, the person you're addressing will probably ask, "What could be a problem?" — and look at that, a peer-to-peer conversation has started.

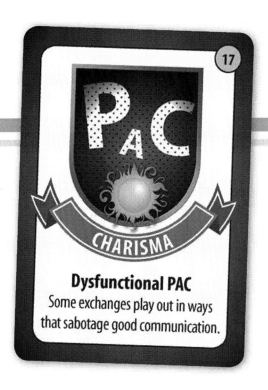

Dysfunctional PAC
Some exchanges play out in ways
that sabotage good communication.

Dysfunctional PAC

The Parent-Adult-Child model of Transactional Analysis can play out in various dysfunctional ways that get in the way of good communication.

The person with a large Parent Ego State and a much smaller Adult and Child is probably a person who doesn't know how to relate to someone if he or she isn't "talking down" to the other person. The person with an oversized Parent Ego State often won't even be able to relate to you unless you're willing to have them "parent you." It might either be nurturing (which can be smothering) or critical (which can be demoralizing). But it will be parenting!

What about the situation where within an individual there's a small Parent (P), a small Adult (A), and a big Child (C). Here, a seven year old runs life. There is very little self-discipline, very little self-control. This person is likely to be impulsive and fearful — everything a seven year old would be.

How about if you have a large P, a small A, and a large C? Most people I work with in my Executive Coaching sessions look like that. They have continued to "raise" themselves after their parents quit raising them. Their Critical Parent continues to try and get their Compliant Child to do the heavy lifting.

Consider the world of sales. The salesperson knows it's time to cold call. And so the Critical Parent inside begins belittling the Child inside–trying to shame the Child into getting up in the chair and making those cold calls.

"What are you afraid of? They're not going to kill you. Get going. What's that? You don't want to? Wimp!" Any seven year old would be afraid of cold calling, but the Parent eventually coerces the child into the chair to make the cold calls.

This person doesn't understand that there is an Adult Ego State within him who will understand much more about cold calling than a seven year old could ever comprehend. How much better an idea it would be to nurture the Child rather than threaten! "I see you're scared of cold calling. Why don't you stay here. I (that would be the Adult) need to go make some cold calls." This would be a much healthier internal conversation.

Great leaders know (intuitively or otherwise) that the Adult Ego State needs to be exercised. In fact, exercising the Adult is one of the best leadership exercises you can do. Standing in front of a mirror, work hard at saying things without any emotion. During this exercise, there is no emotion allowed, not even a curled lip! I find you can say almost anything to anyone when you speak with no emotion from the Adult.

Practice this ego state so that you can access the ego state that's appropriate for any given communication. Here's a good general rule: When you are tempted to speak from the Critical Parent, go to your Adult instead. However, do try to speak from your Nurturing Parent roughly 70% of the time.

On any given day, you might not be able to find your Nurturing Parent. That's when the words "Help me understand" become important. That word track is the battle cry of the Nurturing Parent. "Help me understand how that happened." "Help me understand what was going on when that occurred." "Help me understand why you're bringing this up." The Nurturing Parent often has to begin with such a word script (i.e., behaviorally). No problem. Lead from your behavior.

The Parent, the Adult, and the Child are three key components of who you are — and who everyone else is. I have found this to be a useful model for better understanding how I can connect more effectively with other people in my leadership role.

Actions vs. Words

L eaders often have to figure out what's really going on. When looking for the truth, pay less attention to a person's words than to his or her actions.

It's all too easy to get caught up in words. We say things for many different reasons, and not all of those reasons have the purest of intent.

When I watch a person's actions in my own "search for truth," I am more apt to find out what's actually taking place. When a person's words contradict his or her actions, the actions always tell me truth.

A leader understands that listening to his followers' words is not as significant a source of information as observing his followers' actions.

However, the reverse is also true. Be aware that your followers will be watching your actions far more than they listen to your words. This places a high level of responsibility on the leader. You must be a role model in terms of everything that you want your followers to do and be.

Networking

The larger your network, the more successful you will be at fulfilling responsibilities.

CHARISMA

19

Networking

As leaders, we delegate. We have to. We delegate authority and we set the authority boundaries inside of which our direct reports need to work.

But here's what we know to be true. Many times our own job responsibilities are going to extend beyond our authority boundaries. (And of course, it's the same for our direct reports.) So, for example, I have responsibilities for a particular project. However, I usually don't have authority to go and directly change everything that has to do with successfully accomplishing my responsibilities. This is a fact of business life.

In my experience, there's always a gap between our authority and our ultimate responsibilities. That gap is filled with networking. Here's where we need to get better as a leader in making connections with other people–building a network that can help us fulfill our responsibilities when those responsibilities extend outside our authority boundary.

How do you quickly gain others' trust so that your network becomes larger and larger, and you can successfully fulfill all of your responsibilities (even those that lie outside of your authority boundaries)? Everything you've learned in this section of the book about Charisma will need to come into play.

A Lot to Get Past
How easy is it to get
to know you?

A Lot To Get Past

"So-and-so is a lot to get past" is often a comment made about someone. Usually that means that they aren't easy to get to know. Sometimes it's the fact that they're too quiet and it's like "pulling teeth" to get any information out of them. Sometimes it's the opposite. They're overbearing and talk too much.

Experience has shown that seldom will any of us as individuals be able to accurately judge whether or not we are a lot to get past.

Every leader needs to have around him or her a trusted Board of Advisors who will speak truth into his or her life—telling him or her honestly when he or she is being too much. After all, when a person is a lot to get past, most people just plain won't take the time. A potentially beneficial relationship will be lost.

Who are members of your trusted Board of Advisors? Don't count on your followers to tell you the truth. They may feel like they have too much to lose if they make you unhappy.

People Skills are your ability
to "read" people and influence
them based on your impressions.

TRANSFORMATIONAL TOPICS:

- ☐ Intuitive People Skills
- ☐ Wishy-Washy Words
- ☐ Top Eight Communication Dysfunctions
- ☐ Triangulation
- ☐ The Origin of Anger
- ☐ Healthy Acceptance
- ☐ Boundaries
- ☐ Identity vs. Role
- ☐ The Mental Credit Card
- ☐ Profitability of Pain
- ☐ Comfort Zones
- ☐ Not Everyone's Cup of Tea
- ☐ Anxiety
- ☐ Leave Your Child and Your Mother in the Car
- ☐ Cognitive vs. Behavioral

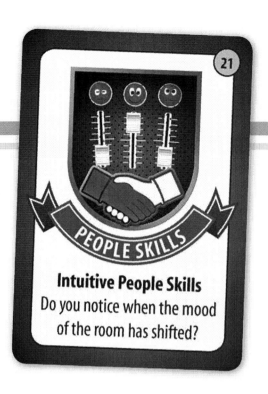

Intuitive People Skills
Do you notice when the mood
of the room has shifted?

Intuitive People Skills

L ots of people think they have good people skills but don't know how to "work a room." In the world of leadership, "people skills" means not just that you can have a good conversation with someone, but also that you are intuitively capable of sensing what's going on in a room, taking the temperature of a group, noticing when the mood of the room has shifted and why. This is not necessarily something you can develop overnight, but it is something for which you can develop a second sense.

Remember: It's not just the words you say. Mastery of "people skills" requires a deep, even instinctive understanding of this point.

Please imagine my wife and me sitting at the breakfast table one Sunday morning. Imagine I'm reading the newspaper. My wife says to me, "Do you love me?" And I say to her in a gruff voice, without taking my eyes off the newspaper, "Yes, I love you."

She still doesn't believe me. My words were right, but she doesn't believe me. So, she asks again, "Do you love me?" I say in a sweet tone, not looking up from the newspaper, "Yes, I love you."

She doesn't believe me. My words are right, and my tone of voice is right. However, I'm going to have to put the paper down. I'm going to have to look at her and say in a loving tone with direct eye contact, "Yes, I love you" if she's going to buy my message. That example shows the power of the non-verbal signals … and the dangers of over-reliance on the "right words." By the way: If I want to be sure my message landed properly, to what do I have to pay attention? You guessed it: Not just her words, not just her tone of voice, but her body language as well.

In growing your intuition as a leader, the understanding of both verbal and non-verbal signals is essential. Ignoring either of those will cause you to lose connection and lose strength. Sometimes, the non-verbal signal takes the form of the rolling of the eyes. Sometimes, it's a sigh. Sometimes, it's just something you sensed, but you never had the confidence to express it and discuss it with the group. Try this: "If you sense it, say it."

Leaders who continue to grow in their leadership role learn to use the phrase, "I sense that… Am I right?" They have the courage to ask that question so that they understand not only the words, but the tone of voice also. They have confidence in their ability to sense non-verbal cues and not ignore them. That's the power of building solid intuition. That's the power of being able to read a room.

PEOPLE SKILLS

Wishy-Washy Words
Are you listening for them?

Wishy-Washy Words

An effective leader has a very finely-tuned listening filter, one that detects and tactfully establishes clarifications for "wishy-washy words."

Words like "probably" or "try" seldom make it through that filter without the leader asking, "When you say 'probably,' what does that mean?" or "Help me understand: What do we want to see finished on this project by this time next week?" Such questions cause the speaker to clarify what is actually meant. What's

73

more, effective leaders know how to send these messages without making their conversational partners feel threatened, judged, or intimidated.

In our sales training sessions, we Sandler trainers speak of salespeople who have "happy ears." These are sellers who give the most optimistic possible "spin" to the wishy-washy words they encounter from prospects, based on what they as sellers want to hear. Sales managers usually nod their heads in recognition when I talk about this, but the truth is, this happens in just about all communications where no effective filter exists.

It's up to us to build and strengthen that filter. The most effective leaders are those who have learned that the optimistic assumptions they make around wishy-washy words never serve them well!

It takes time and practice and tact to build up a "wishy-washy words" filter that leaves people feeling okay about themselves. I suggest a game to make learning this skill more fun. The next time you have a conversation with one of your followers, take notice of how many wishy-washy words you hear. My record is seven for one conversation!

The first step is simply learning to recognize words and phrases that soften commitments and assessments. These are words like ...

- About
- Around
- Roughly
- I'll/We'll try to
- Should

- Maybe
- Something like
- Nearly
- In the neighborhood

Once you begin noticing these words ... start expressing gentle curiosity about what your followers actually mean when they use them!

PEOPLE SKILLS

Top Eight Communication Dysfunctions

Are you communicating ... or trying to get the other person to submit?

Top Eight Communication Dysfunctions

Here are the eight most common baits that people use to get other people into Communication Dysfunctions. This is what happens in dysfunctional interchanges between people.

At their heart, they have one commonality. One person is using his or her strengths against the other person in order to bring that person into submission – so that he or she will acquiesce or come around to a certain way of thinking or acting.

#1. OVERWHELMING.

If I can think faster than you do, then I'm going to outthink you. If I can talk faster than you, then I'm going to outtalk you. If I can emote quicker than you, more than you, then I'm going to out-emote you. I'm going to out-logic you. I'm going to overwhelm you with the sheer force of my personality until I get you to give me what I want. And it's not fair.

#2. UNPLUGGING.

Okay, so I can't dominate you. You know what I'm going to do? I'm going to pull everything in and just unplug from you. This is common in the business meeting where a person pushes his chair away from the table, crosses his arms, folds his legs, and literally turns sideways to the rest of the table. That person has unplugged. That's not fair either.

#3. SARCASM.

You've seen this one in action, haven't you? You share an idea, and someone says: "Oh, well, you *could* do that … if you wanted to ruin the whole company." "What do you mean by that?" you ask. "Oh, I was just joking." Sarcasm is particularly insidious because it has a back door. You can't be called on it, because you can always go out the back door of "I was just kidding." Sarcasm gets the conversation nowhere. It does not move anything forward.

"What did you mean by that?" is about the only response that you can offer to someone's use of sarcasm—bringing that person to where he actually says what he meant rather than cloaking it in sarcasm.

#4. NON-VERBAL CUES.

People don't need words to speak. They can speak with a rolling of the eyes or with a sigh or in dozens of other ways. The only way to combat this dysfunction is to say something like, "Help me out: What did you mean just now? I ask because if I'm left to myself to assume I know what you mean, I usually go 'dark.' I would rather you tell me what you meant when you did that." (And don't go into too much detail about what you mean by "did that." In other words, don't say, "Why did you roll your eyes just now?" Focus on what the person was trying to communicate.)

#5. SUBJECT CHANGING.

Another classic. This one is best combatted before starting a conversation, by having the subject of that conversation already clearly defined. That way, if anything new comes up, you can both agree to put it on hold for another time.*

#6. BLAMING/GUILT.

This cycle can cause massive amounts of time to be wasted in a conversation with no resolution of the situation. It is perhaps the most reliable time-waster on this list.

---

* See card 47, Up-Front Contracts.

#7. NAME CALLING.

This one can be quite tricky. We usually don't realize we're doing it. Frequently, a company will tell me, "We don't allow any name calling around here." I always say: "Oh, I bet you do. You're just sophisticated about how people should go about calling names." I haven't been proved wrong on that yet. Suppose the CEO says something like, "Of course, the intelligent opinion to have is..." What does that mean? It means that anyone else who doesn't have that opinion is not intelligent! That's name calling in a sophisticated fashion.

You can also call someone a name by using a certain tone of voice, "Now, don't you understand that the best way to do this is to..." The person you're talking to can fill in the blank without any difficulty. The missing word is "stupid." You've just name-called.

#8. ATTACKING THE OTHER'S IDENTITY.

This is where we go beyond blaming and guilt and move into the big leagues: shaming. There is a big difference between guilt and shame. "Guilt" is saying, "You made a mistake." Shame is saying, "You are a mistake." They're both dysfunctional, but shame is a much more powerful variety. With shame, we're attacking the other's identity. In essence we're saying they're not worthy of being loved. That is a low blow indeed.

In all of this, it is essential to remember that we teach people how to treat us. When people come to me to complain about how they're being treated, I wait until the end of their complaining and then often say, "You taught them to treat you that way. How are you going to change that?"

What I mean is that they're going to have to put up personal boundaries that prevent these dysfunctions from occurring in their presence, and boundaries that prevent people from using these dysfunctions against them.

A strong leader knows to stay away from these Eight Communication Dysfunctions ... and knows how to call out his or her followers — ideally in private — when they start using them.

24

Triangulation
Don't insert yourself into a situation
that needs to be resolved by others.

PEOPLE SKILLS

Triangulation

Triangulation occurs when the leader inserts himself or herself into a situation that needs to be worked through by the two (or more) parties primarily involved in the situation.

The true leader understands that whenever Triangulation happens, he or she is robbing the parties in question of a learning experience. Rather than stepping in and taking care of the situation for the parties, the most effective leader knows how to intervene with one or more of the parties to explore new ways to approach the situation and resolve the matter without the leader having to "fix it."

That approach creates other leaders. Triangulation, on the other hand, only creates learned dependency on the part of the followers (which is a prison for the leader and one that he or she will eventually regret having created).

The Origin of Anger
What does anger encountered
in the workplace mean?

The Origin
of Anger

With rare exception, anger is always a secondary emotion. It is fueled by the primary emotions of fear or hurt.

To be sure, there are those instances where someone is incensed by injustices done in the world to the point of anger or as it's sometimes called "righteous indignation." However, this is quite rare in the workplace. Most of the time, the anger leaders must deal with is coming from someone who is not comfortable with expressing the emotions of fear or hurt. The person is just more comfortable expressing anger.

A wise leader understands this and looks beyond the anger of the direct report to gain a clearer understanding of the fear or hurt fueling the anger. Addressing that emotion, rather than reacting to the anger, is a universal (and universally admired) trait of great leaders.

A strong leader can express fear and hurt, and doesn't have to substitute anger. Without this ability, a leader will struggle to make sense of his or her own anger, and of the anger expressed by those who follow.

Welcome

PEOPLE SKILLS

Healthy Acceptance
Accept people as they are. Everyone,
including you, has dysfunctions.

Healthy Acceptance

One common battle cry in the workplace is "You need to accept me the way I am." That may be true, but there are healthy and unhealthy approaches to acceptance, and leaders with good people skills know the difference.

The healthy mid-range of acceptance falls in the place where I accept people and understand that everyone, including me, has dysfunctions. What I call the "fringes" of acceptance can be found at the far left and right ends. At the left in the diagram is where I accept people's dysfunctions while disregarding my own personal boundaries.

The Healthy Mid-Range

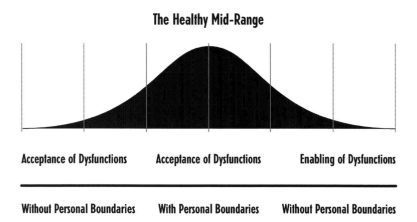

Acceptance of Dysfunctions	Acceptance of Dysfunctions	Enabling of Dysfunctions
Without Personal Boundaries	With Personal Boundaries	Without Personal Boundaries

Let's use a bizarre dysfunction to illustrate the difference I'm talking about. Suppose someone insists on spitting. It's just a habit. They spit wherever they go. I accept that as a dysfunction. It's a sad dysfunction that they have to spit wherever they go, but I accept that about them.

However, I happen to have personal boundaries which say, "Please do not spit around me."

Isn't everyone allowed the right to have personal boundaries like that? Think of it physically. You have a boundary. You don't want someone to lean into your face and be a "close talker." You have a range of area in which you want people to stand when they're talking to you.

When people get too close, and try to talk to you, that's uncomfortable. Then again, if they stand too far away when they try to talk to you, that's uncomfortable, too. There are boundaries that you, as a human being, are able and authorized to set for yourself.

The far right end of this particular bell-shaped curve, which I call the Acceptance Curve, is where I go if I want to *enable* the dysfunctions of others. So now, not only does this person have a problem with spitting, I enable that problem. I say, "Here, let me bring you a spittoon." I encourage it.

"Healthy Acceptance" is found in the middle. It's the place where I understand we all have dysfunctions, but I don't allow you to act out your dysfunctions on me. I have personal boundaries that I put up to protect me. That's my right as an individual. Anything else ends up being toxic.

The point here is that **all acceptance is not created equal.** Great leaders understand that sometimes, in accepting their followers, they are doing themselves and their followers no favors. The great leader accepts the fact that we are all flawed, and accepts the fact that we are all imperfect — without compromising his or her own personal boundaries.

Boundaries
Establish and defend
personal boundaries.

Boundaries

L ook at the diagram on the following page. Notice that one of the boxes is a solid line. The other is a dotted line.

What that means is that someone doesn't have their boundaries clearly defined, and consequently it's easy for the other party to violate those boundaries and step in where they are not wanted. This causes the "violator" to lose respect for the person who allows his or her boundaries to be violated.

Consider the situation where a woman, who typically values

workplace relationships for their own sake more than the man does, allows her boundaries concerning receiving personal credit for work performed to become a "dotted line" for the sake of keeping the working relationship going. She compromises more; she accommodates more than the man does. Consequently, the man ultimately loses respect for her as a colleague.

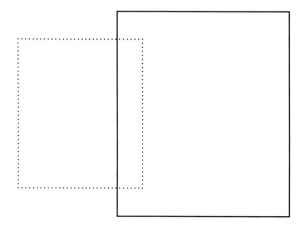

This is not an uncommon pattern, whereas a man tends to believe he can push his way forward to what he wants; a woman depends on relationships in order to achieve that which she desires. In most cases, she values relationships more than men do, and consequently she more likely allows such boundaries to be violated more than men. So there may be some work do to there in terms of learning to defend one's boundaries. **Leaders do not operate with dotted lines as their boundaries.**

Let's put it in a physical context. If somebody came by and kicked the back of your chair every morning as they came to work, how long would it take you to say, "That's not acceptable"? Twice? Three times? One time? How long will it take you to say, "That's not acceptable," when you're called out in an insulting way in a public meeting? How long would it take for you to say, "That's not acceptable," when passed over for another promotion in favor of someone with lesser credentials?

These are all boundary issues.

A strong leader knows where his or her boundaries are and doesn't allow people to violate them—realizing that sometimes this will put the relationship at risk. A strong leader encourages his or her followers to do the same.

I encourage you to order the book entitled *Boundaries* by Dr. Henry Cloud if you believe you could benefit from more information on this important topic.

PEOPLE SKILLS

Identity vs. Role
Role is what you do.
Identity is who you are.

Identity vs. Role

ole is what you do. Identity is who you are. In the chart on the next page, you'll see a thermometer-type vertical axis with numbers between zero and 10, and two columns.

On any given day in my role, I can feel like I'm performing at zero ... or I can feel like I'm performing at 10.

On any given day in my identity, I can feel like zero about who I am ... or I can feel like 10 about who I am.

Unfortunately, many people go through life with no line

down the middle. They do not separate who they are from what
they do.

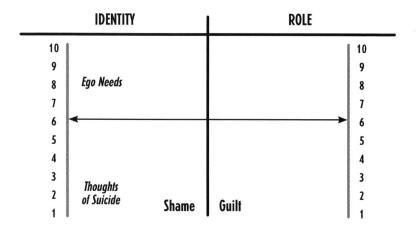

I want you to pause for a moment and think about the problems that occur when you are not separating who you are from
what you do. On any given day, as you do better in your role, you
feel better about yourself. On any given day, as you do worse in
your role, you feel worse about yourself.

You are on a roller coaster of feelings about yourself based on
your performance. You're constantly driven to keep the line up on
the right side so that you can feel good about yourself. But all the
good feeling is performance-based.

I noticed this with my dad. I don't know if he ever had a line
down the middle. In the later years of his life, he had Parkinson's
Disease. If I had come up to him and said, "How do you feel about
yourself, Dad?" He would have said, "I don't feel very good about
myself. I can't do what I used to be able to do. If someone came
to hurt your mom, I couldn't protect her. I don't provide for you
and the family like I used to either." And I would have said, "Dad,
that's what you do. You're still valuable as a person (who you are)."

I'm not sure if he ever had that line between his identity and his role. My hope for you is that you do.

Let me take a moment to explore some of the problems that can happen to you as a leader if you don't have that line.

If you look at the left side, you'll see, "Here's how I feel about myself from zero to 10." On any given day let's say I function at 6. That's my sense of OK-ness about myself. I feel okay about myself at about a 6.

The gap between 6 and 10 is what we call our "ego needs." So, I need to get myself feeling better about myself by about 4 points every day.

Have you ever met someone you identified as having a "big ego?" A person who's all about himself or herself? I'm talking about those people who always have to talk about themselves and make the conversation come back to them. They tend to have large ego needs, which is different from having a "big ego." They might have been functioning in the 4s or 3s in terms of their typical feelings about themselves.

And so, we erroneously use the term, "He or she has a big ego," when actually, the person just has a large set of ego needs. People try to fill those ego needs with their performance. Well, on some days they will get closer than others.

Here's what I know about that left line. I can't let it get below 2, because when I start feeling that poorly about myself, thoughts of suicide come in. I start thinking things like, "I'd be better off gone." "The world would be better off with me gone." "The people around me would be better off if I got out of here." "I'm more trouble than I'm worth."

I know I can't let myself go there. Consequently, I find myself having to keep the thermometer higher than 2. How do I do that?

Well, that's a challenge. If I don't have a line between my identity and my role, and someone comes to me with what I perceive as negative feedback, it passes right by my role and shoots straight into my identity. I feel like they're trying to drag me down as a person, and I inevitably become defensive. They're pushing my thermometer in the wrong direction.

This is why defensive people tend to be people with a very low score on the left side of this chart. When you give them any constructive feedback, they can't keep that feedback on the right side, which is where it belongs. You're just telling them about their role, but it goes straight to the left side, which is where they house their identity, and defensiveness sets in. They don't want to drop any lower on that important scale than they already are.

Leaders who are defensive are really difficult to follow, because they aren't open to any kind of meaningful feedback. They aren't open to input from their followers. So, they become quite dictatorial in what amounts to an extremely insecure leadership style.

How, do the left and the right columns affect each other? I think they do, even with the line in place. **I tend to perform on the right in keeping with the level that I feel on the left.**

So suppose I have a really great day. Since I work so much with salespeople, let's say I'm a salesperson, and I make a big sale. I come home at night. I'm taking my socks off on the edge of the bed. And I say to myself, "Wow! That was great to get that sale. I'm good ...but I'm not that good."

And the next day, I'll begin to function back around that 6 line.

What's happening is that I tend to function on the right side of the line in a way that reflects how I feel about myself on the left. It's really difficult to perform higher and stay higher than how I feel about myself on the left.

When I perform poorly or I do something that I know to be wrong, I feel guilt. I made a mistake. We all have those feelings.

Shame is significantly different. Guilt is "I made a mistake." Shame is "I am a mistake."

My worthiness, my ability to feel worthy of being loved, comes into question when the left side gets low. So, the natural question is, "How do I keep the score on the left side of this chart high?" Well, some people find that their faith does that. If they believe in a God who loves them for who they are, they already have a foundation on which to build.

Others find that it's keeping a balance in their life. They notice that some people try to get too much out of work, and some people try to get too much out of a relationship, trying to get their identity to come up to a 10 with just one part of life. They realize it doesn't work that way. It's the balance of life that allows us to find ourselves most refreshed on the left side of the equation.

When I get home after a day of work, and my grandchildren are excited to see me when I walk through the door, that helps me to balance out whatever happened at work that day. Some people might be able to get the same kind of lift by participating in a weekly bowling league. That might work if I weren't lucky enough to have grandkids who lived nearby, a loving wife, and a loving family! But if I don't have social interactions, if I don't have other outlets besides work, then I will try to get my whole sense of self-worth, my whole sense of worthiness of being loved, from work. That's doomed to failure. Work can't deliver. We all need balance.

The key point to understand is that we really do need to have a line down the middle between our identity and our role. And once that line is drawn, you really do need to defend it.

When I work with managers, and I'm talking to them about their performance reviews with their direct reports, I encourage them to actually take out a piece of paper, draw this two-column chart, and talk explicitly about the fact that what you're about to say has nothing to do with the person's value as an individual. "Your value as a human being is not under discussion." Say those words, or something very close to them, right out loud!

By having this kind of discussion, you'll make it as clear as you can possibly make it that you're going to be speaking to the right side of this two-column chart. Hand the direct report the sheet of paper and ask them to take their notes from the performance review on the right side of the two-column chart. And then, when it's over, ask them how they're feeling. Remind them that they're still at 10 over on the left side!

You may not be used to having a discussion like this. But if you're interested in building up your people skills, you'll get used to it! I believe it's a manager's job to protect the identity of their direct reports. **Protect the identity and coach to the role.**

The Mental Credit Card
You can't store painful experiences
in the "back room" forever.

The Mental Credit Card

his card portrays what I believe happens in the human mind as positive experiences and negative experiences enter it.

When we're young, we don't have the equipment for dealing with sharp, painful experiences. Consequently, we tend to metaphorically put them "behind a wall" in the back of our minds–trying to ignore them. As we continue this practice, the amount of "stuff" hidden behind that wall grows. As we grow older, though, we may have trouble holding the wall in place as efficiently as we once did.

Most people can continue to put painful experiences in that back pantry well into their 30s. However, at some point, the sharp, painful experiences start to pop over the wall, through the door, and land in the front of the mind. At that point, the adult is older and (we hope) has more and better equipment for dealing with the painful experiences. In the best case scenario, grown-ups can work their way through the bad stuff and leave those out in front of the wall. Alternatively, they could attempt to just put them back behind the wall. There is a storage fee for doing that. You may not be able to afford to keep storing everything in the back room forever. You may max out your mental credit card.

Entire marriages have been built on mental credit cards. Eventually the day comes when the payment comes due and both parties look at each other sadly, realizing the back room is so full that even the thought of working through a fraction of it in one lifetime is insurmountable. Often, divorce becomes the option of choice.

A good leader seeks to keep short accounts on the "mental credit card." A leader seeks to keep mental energy from being dissipated by items kept behind the wall, and by the effort needed to keep the wall up. A leader seeks to come to terms with old issues and deal with new issues as they arise so his or her mind can remain clear, and energy can be invested in more profitable pursuits.

Profitability of Pain
It is not your job to protect
your followers from pain.

Profitability of Pain

I believe, as leaders, we can often succumb to the myth that our job is to protect our followers from pain. However, as we chart out our own lives, I believe some insights can come our way that help us overcome this myth.

Imagine a line that represents your life. You are a newborn baby at the beginning of the line, and your tombstone's at the end. On that line you placed a star indicating where you are in your life right now. Then you charted your three to five highlights in your life. The higher the dot above the line, the bigger the thrill of that particular high. You would also then chart your three to five low points.

You plotted those out and then you wrote above the line and off to the right, "What I learned from my highs." There you wrote out everything that your successes gave you in terms of lessons learned. Then, below the line and off to the right, you wrote "What I learned from my lows." In that space, you wrote out everything your lows taught you about yourself and about life.

You told the truth. And what did you notice?

I have been helping people conduct this exercise for decades. I have yet to see a situation where more wasn't learned from the lows than from the highs. Everybody who charts this out seems to come to the same conclusion. The strongest lessons, the lessons that stayed with them the longest, the lessons that went into their long-term memory, the lessons that literally and permanently changed their behaviors for the better, usually came from the lowest moments!

So, for us as leaders to protect our followers from the pain that can change them for the better is to actually do them a disservice. The best leaders know beyond any shadow of a doubt that there is profit in pain. They know that rescuing their followers from pain is a strategy that deprives them of learning (which is the opposite of what they want for their followers or for the organization as a whole).

People Skills

Comfort Zones
Engage with that which
makes you uncomfortable.

Comfort Zones

There's "that place where the magic happens." And then there's our comfort zones. There is no intersection between those two places.

We all have comfort zones. We are all surrounded by fear. That means we have comfort zones in relation to the emotions we are willing to express, the situations we are willing to put ourselves into, the countries to which we are willing to travel, and a thousand other such limitations.

We have comfort zones on all different levels.

What great leaders understand is that in order for them to grow in terms of their own influence as a leader, or in terms of the number of people they can lead, or in terms of the breadth of situations into which they can lead those people, they themselves have to expand their comfort zone.

They do that by walking through that barrier of fear that surrounds every comfort zone we have. Someone once said, "Courage is doing it scared." A great leader understands that.

Not Everyone's Cup of Tea
Accept that you won't please everyone
with the decisions you make and
the principles you hold.

Not Everyone's Cup of Tea

This one comes from my wife. I like how it sounds: Not everyone is going to like me.

That's reality!

Often, when I encourage people to seek counseling, I say, "You need to visit several counselors because you may not fit with the first one you visit." When people are asking for help in finding the right church, I say, "You may need to visit many churches, because you may not fit with the first church you visit."

No one is everyone's cup of tea. An effective leader understands that. Not everyone will follow any given leader because that leader may not be everyone's cup of tea. And to accept that and to embrace that is to set onseself free from the burden of trying to meet everyone's expectations.

Have you noticed? Great leaders carry themselves with an understanding that they won't please everyone with the decisions that they make, with the directions that they take, with the principles that they hold. They continue to resolutely lead anyway.

Anxiety

Everyone suffers from periodic bouts of situational anxiety. Those who suffer from a state of perpetual anxiety are different because they're the ones who tend to make two very common thinking mistakes.

First, they ignore the true statistical probability of an event's occurrence. Consequently, for someone who experiences frequent anxiety, it is equally probable to them that they will arrive at their destination safely or that they will die on the way. The two possible perceived outcomes are perceived as more or less equally likely, even though reliable statistics indicate that many more people arrive safely at their destinations than die on the way.

Secondly, they catastrophize the results of anything happening. "If this or that happened, it would be the worst possible thing that could ever occur in my career/the company's history/the history of mankind." So their thinking goes.

Both of these thinking flaws will keep their amygdala (the fear center of the brain) in constant operation – flooding their system with all the physiological chemical alarms – signaling danger on a primal level.

The leader understands that these two anxiety-producing thoughts must be labeled as flawed thinking whenever they arise, and must be managed consciously to help lower anxiety and maintain the clear thinking that supports important decision making.

Leave Your Child and Your Mother in the Car

When it's time to do an Adult job, leave the Critical Parent and the Child out of it.

Leave Your Child and Your Mother in the Car

One voice sounds like the voice of a seven year old with all the fears, doubts, and impulsiveness you would expect from a child that age. One sounds like the voice of a critical parent, telling you what you can and can't do with your capabilities and lack thereof.

This card reminds us that when effective leaders need to do an

Adult job, they leave the Critical Parent and the Child out of it. The Adult component inside the leader had better go have the difficult conversation (the Child will be too scared); the Adult component inside the leader had better go and visit with the CEO (the Parent won't believe the leader is worthy of the CEO's time); and the Adult component inside the leader had better be the messenger of any bad news (since neither the Parent nor Child wants to be anywhere near a potentially explosive situation).

Just leave them both in the car so one can watch over the other. They'll only get in the way of you being as courageous and confident as you need to be.*

---

* See card 16, Transactional Matters, for more details on these interior self-limiting voices.

Cognitive vs. Behavioral
Thoughts affect behavior,
and vice versa.

Cognitive vs. Behavioral

Psychologists typically fall into one of two camps. You'll hear some saying, "We'll change the way you behave by changing the way you think." They're the cognitive psychologists. The other group is saying to them, "We'll change the way you think by changing the way you behave." They're the behavioral psychologists.

The truth is, it's not either/or, but both/and. A wise leader knows when to incorporate which approach. Many times, I can't wait for my thinking (or that of my direct reports) to change. I must begin behaving differently before I start thinking differently.

My dad had a poster that he'd hung in the garage. I don't know why it was in the garage. It said, "If you want to be enthusiastic, act enthusiastic." And the truth is, many times, we have to start behaving before our feelings will catch up with us. And so, we start behaving in a certain manner and our feelings come along for the ride. We start behaving more confident than we feel, and pretty soon we have confidence.

On the other hand, our feelings really are a result of our thoughts. Every feeling that I have has a thought behind it. When I don't feel confident, there's a thought that's lingering there, fueling my feelings. If my feelings are a pot of water, the fire that's causing it to boil are my thoughts. I need to get in control of those thoughts and replace them with new thoughts in order to control my emotions and thereby change my behaviors.

So, my advice to leaders is to use both approaches with yourself and with your direct reports. Help people grab hold of their thoughts; help them become accountable to themselves for those thoughts; and help them think about what's causing them to behave in a certain manner. At the same time, you should also know that to wait until you're fully confident before you ever do anything will mean that nothing ever happens. Sometimes, you just have to do it and then get confidence through your actions. That's the behavioral side.

Leaders understand that those two schools of thought are not in conflict with each other. They're complementary.

Courage is your ability to feel secure in a situation and make others feel secure.

TRANSFORMATIONAL TOPICS:

- ☐ The Confidence Paradox
- ☐ Social Masks
- ☐ Intimidation
- ☐ The Reality Room
- ☐ Left Brain, Right Brain
- ☐ Control

The Confidence Paradox
Don't wait until confidence
appears. Take action.

The Confidence Paradox

magine someone looking onto a stage from the wings. Someone who wants to go on stage and speak to the group that's sitting – waiting – for the big speech. This person is thinking, "I will wait here backstage until I feel confident enough to walk onto that stage."

Unfortunately, that's not how confidence occurs.

I could go backstage and work with this person on all the preparation–taking the speaker-in-waiting from timid up to where he or she felt prepared. I could teach the person how to open the speech, how to close it, and how to organize all the points in between.

The paradox about confidence, though, is that this speaker-in-waiting would still have to take that first step … without really feeling all that confident. That's what it takes to build confidence. **If we wait to feel confident before we are willing to step onto that stage, we will spend the rest of our lives waiting backstage.** Guess what? Real confidence (in this case the ability to speak effectively and confidently in front of a group) comes only after you've taken some kind of action. In this situation, the change has to be behavioral. You do have to do something, even though you don't always feel particularly confident as you begin.

At some point, we have to walk through our fear. We have to walk to the center of that stage and address the people. Then when we leave the stage, we will have begun to close the gap between preparation and total confidence.

Remember: "Courage is doing it scared." I don't believe confidence comes any other way. A true leader understands this.

COURAGE

Social Masks
Comparisons with others are likely to be inaccurate and/or create complacency.

Social Masks

Whenever they find themselves comparing themselves to others (something that just about all of us do from time to time) great leaders are careful to avoid two common traps.

First, they remind themselves that we are seldom if ever comparing "apples to apples."

Most of the time, we are comparing what we believe to be true about ourselves to the other person's "Social Mask." We all have one of those masks. It's the person we show to the public. Only those in our most intimate relationships get to see us mask-free.

Consequently, we can create all types of self-doubt by wondering why our career isn't as advanced as theirs, why our spouse isn't as kind as theirs, why our children aren't as obedient as theirs, and so on. We build unrealistic pictures in our minds that are based on the social image someone presents. These pictures, which may have no basis at all in the life the person actually lives on a daily basis, can stir extreme self-doubt if we let them. In 1961, most of the people in the United States thought John and Jackie Kennedy led an idyllic family life, and many couples compared themselves unfavorably to the image of the Kennedys' supposedly perfect marriage. We know now that the picture was a far more complex and painful one than the pretty magazine photos led the country to believe.

On the other side of the coin, leaders understand that comparison can also create complacency ... for as long as you view yourself doing better than someone else is. So for instance: You might still not be using all of your giftedness to bring value to life, but you comfort yourself with the thought that at least you're doing better than "Wally" is. This kind of thinking is an obstacle to continued growth, and effective leaders know that.

Comparing yourself to others is a natural human tendency, but it seldom delivers positive results.

Intimidation
Build a rebuttal to your internal
Critical Parent's pessimism.

Intimidation

I love the story Jay Leno tells of his mother saying to him, "Jay, you better learn how to dance because you're just not that funny." Can't you just hear a parent saying that?

In the world of sales, we have a saying: "You can only call as high in a company as your mother will let you." (It could be your dad, for that matter.)

Our internal Critical Parent has a way of saying things like, "Who do you think you are, calling on the President of the company?" "Why do you think he would want to hear anything from you?" "Who do you think you are, talking to someone who's that much more successful than you, who has that much more money than you do, who's that much older than you, who has that much more beauty than you?" "Don't get too big for your britches!"

Most of these are internal conversations, and they tend to be pretty one-sided. But just like when we left home, there comes a time when we have to stand up straight and talk back: "It's time for you to be quiet Mom (or Dad). You're way off on your perception of me and you're way off on your perception of others."

In my particular case, it was wealth. When I was growing up, my mother was always talking about people who live in the "Country Club" neighborhood. Whenever she said that, I knew she wasn't talking about us. And she said it in such a way that I knew that "Country Club" people were significantly different than us. So when I grew up, I was always intimidated by those who earned more money than I did. In fact, wealth was my primary intimidation factor.

However, there did come a day when I turned to my mom inside of myself and I said to that internal voice, "Mom, it's time for you to be quiet. You did not understand those people who live in Country Club. I'm discovering they are far more like you and me than they are different. There are rich people with problems. There are middle-class people with problems. We're all people."

Once I talked back to her, she quit trying to convince me they were different. I was able to overcome (for the most part) my intimidation of people of wealth. My hope is that this insight works for you in the areas that might be intimidating you and holding you back as a leader.

You might need some time to build an argument to serve as a rebuttal to your mother's words. After all, those words have been coming at you for a long time. Take the time to collect what that Critical Parent says to you and write down why you now believe those words are false. In the calm of the moment, you can write the words so that you can use the rebuttal when you need it. Critical Parents were very influential in our lives as children, but we need to lose their influence as we mature in our leadership responsibilities.

The Reality Room
Truth hurts sometimes, but it beats trying to live according to lies.

The Reality Room

When I'm in the Reality Room, sometimes I succeed, sometimes I fail; sometimes I'm good, sometimes I'm bad; sometimes I'm sick, sometimes I'm well; sometimes I make money, sometimes I lose money – and so on. That's where emotionally healthy people live most of their life.

Parents have a job: To usher a child who's born totally outside the Reality Room *into* the Reality Room. It takes years.

Think of it. When you're born, people take care of you, feed you, change your diaper. In fact, people take care of all your needs and pay all your bills for a long, long time.

This is not the world of adult reality. Parents who are doing their job will gradually usher a child into the Reality Room.

Most of us were shocked as we got out into the world as it was. The Reality Room was not what we were used to. And let's face it: Our parents couldn't get the job of transitioning us while we were living in their house, under their roof, with them supplying the food on the table and the housing.

For most of us, our parents couldn't get us into the Reality Room on their own. Somewhere along the line, Reality itself helped.

Some people fight being in the Reality Room. They like sitting outside the Reality Room instead. Leaders need to learn to recognize those people. Here's why: Usually, they're hoping you're going to help them stay outside the Reality Room. They don't like it in there. But here's the truth. Reality always wins.

I could look at the wall in the Reality Room and I could say, "I want to leave this room. There shouldn't even be a Reality Room." I could throw myself against the wall over and over and over again, but that doesn't mean the walls of the Reality Room are going to come down. Reality is reality.

You might also call this room the Room of Truth. Truth hurts sometimes, but it beats trying to live in the Room of Lies. Living in the Reality Room really is the least stressful option.

Some people have one foot in the Reality Room and one foot out of the Reality Room. True leaders embrace the reality of their situation and make the most of wherever they find themselves.

A wise person once said, "You can't solve a problem unless you first acknowledge it." If you're trying to ignore reality or live outside of reality or make up rules that don't fit reality, your life is going to be more stressed than it should be.

By the same token, if you're helping other people live outside the Reality Room, your life is going to be more stressed than it needs to be.

Emotionally healthy people live in the Reality Room and learn to cope there.

Now what's interesting about the newer generation entering the workplace is that their parents were the first in our history to see the world as a profoundly unsafe place. I'm generalizing a little here, but I think you can see where I'm going. When I was a kid, my parents would say, "Go on out and play. When the streetlights come on make sure you come in." I was on my own. Can you imagine someone saying that to a kid in New York City, or Chicago, or Los Angeles today?

The new generation that's entering the workplace today is the most protected in modern history.

In their defense, their parents had good reason to see the world as unsafe. The result? Many of today's younger were "hovered over" in a way that other workers weren't. That means the trip they have to take from the protective world of Home all the way out to the Reality Room is even longer than the trip that other workplace generations have had to make.

As managers who work with the newer generation, you have to remember that you will be part parent. Whether you like it or not, you are likely to have to put in some time finishing the job that the parents didn't quite get done — bringing the direct report completely into the Reality Room. The good news is that a lot of these younger workers — in my experience, a clear majority — really want to be mentored by more experienced people. (That wasn't necessarily true of, say, the Baby Boomer generation in which I grew up.)

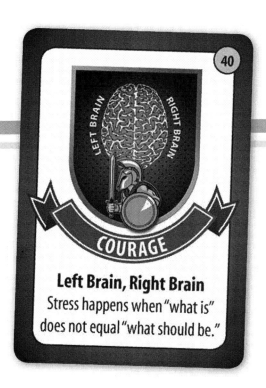

Left Brain, Right Brain

Those who study brain function tell us that the right brain is where our feelings and emotions are most likely to arise. The left side is where our rational and logical function is most likely to arise.

When those two come into conflict, we feel stress. It has been my experience that the left brain, (that logical part of us), often talks to us in terms of what "should be." The right side of the brain, often talks in terms of "what is."

I remember how squeamish I was, years ago, about taking my children out in public because they were so honest about "what was." We'd be standing, talking to somebody and suddenly they'd say, "That person has bad breath." And the person was still standing right next to me! I would have to take them aside and say, "We don't do that. You shouldn't have said that while the person was still there." The left brain came in. The child was so honest.

When my left brain and my right brain are in agreement, I don't have stress. When my left brain and my right brain are supporting each other, there is no stress. But you know what? That's not always the way it goes.

This morning, I stood in front of a mirror. I looked at myself. I said, "Dave, you have a fairly large nose." Fortunately, this morning, the Nurturing Parent came forward and said, "You *should* have a large nose. Your grandmother had a large nose. Your mother had a large nose. It runs in your family. It makes sense that you would have a fairly large nose."

OK, I was at peace. Had I weighed in with, "No, you shouldn't have a large nose," I would have begun to stress.

Think about those situations in life in which you experience stress. I think you will find that it usually has something to do with your circumstances not equaling what part of you believes should be happening.

My car is at the head of a line of traffic, waiting to merge onto the freeway. Yet another car already on the freeway has passed me at the speed of light. It feels like about a hundred cars like that have gone past. Each of them passed a sign telling them that it was time to merge. Yet they all shifted into hyper speed and continue *not* to merge. Part of me screams inside, "They shouldn't do that."

"What is" happening does not equal what I believe "should be," and I start feeling stress. I have a moment of irritation over that event.

This is all good news because it means stress is not some force outside of ourselves. It's not a great cloud that suddenly comes over us and settles down on us.

Between every situation and every feeling of stress, there's a thought. If I were carrying dishes from the table, and I dropped one and it broke on the floor, and I felt stressed, it wasn't the breaking dish that caused me to feel stress. It was my thought about the breaking dish that caused me to feel stress. Maybe I said to myself, "You shouldn't have done that." "What's the matter with you?" "You're stupid." "You're clumsy."

That conversation might have started automatically, but it was the cause of the stress I felt. When I broke the dish, I thought to myself some variation of this thought: "I shouldn't have done that."

Stress is what happens when "what is" does not equal what I believe "should be". The good news is if I can capture that thought, and I can think it through, then I can actually dismantle, overcome, reverse-engineer my stress.

There are three simple rules that I have found help immensely with stress reduction.

#1. SEPARATE YOUR STANDARDS FROM YOUR EXPECTATIONS.

Know the difference between the two. If you really want to manage your stress, your standards cannot equal your expectations.

Here's an example: What are my standards for my children? My standards are pretty simple. My children should not lie to me (that's the left side of my brain).

My children should not lie to me. I've made that clear to them.

What are my expectations for my children? My children are in fact going to lie to me. If my standards and my expectations have never been separated, that produces stress.

Standards come from some external source from which I pull my values and morals. And I say, "Here are the standards." And I'm going to try not to deviate from those standards. You don't have to deviate from your standards. But my expectations come from getting to know another person and reasonably setting expectations for that person, in the light of who that person has proved to be in the real world.

I don't have the same expectations for some people that I do for others. My standards do not vary. Stress is produced when I don't have a clear separation of my standards from my expectations, when I mistake one for the other.

#2. LEARN TO SAY, "THAT'S NOT MY PROBLEM."

I don't mean that in a cavalier manner. And I don't mean it in a way that would cause you to act like you don't care. What I mean is, effective leaders understand what is their problem and what isn't their problem. When we take on problems that aren't ours, when we try to solve problems for other people, we are not operating in the real world.

The reality is, "You have problems, and I have problems." Reality in physical terms might be "I have a yard, and you have a yard." There's a lot line. I keep my yard mowed, and you keep your yard mowed. I can offer you help if you happen to be sick, but it's your responsibility to keep your yard mowed. It's your problem to keep your yard mowed. Not mine.

#3. QUIT TRYING TO MAKE OTHERS' WORLDS THE WAY THEY WANT THEM TO BE.

Many people would like to live much or all of their lives outside the real world that strong leaders inhabit. They don't want to assume personal responsibility for circumstances, or embrace those circumstances. They want someone else to come along and take care of everything for them. Whenever you choose not to enable such people, it is likely that they are going to be irritated with you. However, before you get into some kind of negative cycle with that person, stop and think about what an irritation really is.

An irritation could be something as simple as you not meeting the other person's expectations. Well, people have all kinds of expectations! Does it mean that the expectations are reasonable? Let's be honest: expectations can be pretty dysfunctional. Someone you report to could be looking at you saying, "Here, I need this done by tomorrow at noon." They hand you a sheet of paper that says, "Dismantle and reassemble the Brooklyn Bridge." Then they turn and walk away. Five minutes later, someone who reports to you could hand you a sheet of paper that says, "Make me the CEO of the company in three months." They turn around and walk away, too.

They want their world to work so that no matter when they gave it to you, no matter how much they gave to you, you are supposed to make it so they can say "it's done" at noon tomorrow, or three months from now, or whenever.

Quit trying to make other people's worlds the way they want them to be. Quit trying to alter reality for others. If you could, then sure, you would. You just don't have that much power.

Yes. There's going to be friction sometimes. People are going to go through the stages of grief as they lose something they want.

There is going to be denial, bargaining, anger, depression, and, eventually, acceptance of the fact that you're holding the line on the way things really work.

Don't give up as they go through those various stages. Don't sell yourself out and don't sell the other person out! Both of you live in the real world, and the sooner both of you come to terms with that, the better off everyone is going to be. The way we say it is: "We teach others how to treat us." If you don't like the way you're being treated by somebody, take responsibility for that. You taught them to treat you that way, and you can teach them differently.

Re-train them, tactfully. This will take time. It will take persistence. It will take consistency on your part. But you'll watch your stress levels come down once you both begin living in the reality-based community.

41

COURAGE

Control
Focus on personal objectives to connect
the parts of your life you can affect.

Control

H ere's what might be a helpful exercise. Make a two-column
chart. List on the left side what you are absolutely sure are
totally under your control. On the right side, list as many
things as you can think of that you don't control. Keep writing for
five straight minutes.

This is a very revealing exercise, and it's one I urge you to do
at your earliest opportunity. If you're like me, you'll find the left
column has a very short list. I can control my thoughts. I can con-

trol my feelings. And I can control my behaviors. That's about it. Everything else goes on the right hand side. That means I've got a lot that I could fear.

As a leader, I must focus on what I can control (i.e., my thoughts, my feelings, my behaviors). And on a good day I really do exercise that control over those elements. That's where I need to focus my attention.

Think about how often we create goals around things we don't control. How much better off would we be if we were to make goals around those things we do control? Things we *can* actually affect: our thoughts, our feelings, our behaviors.

Once you start training your mind to focus increasingly on personal objectives that connect to the components of your life you really can control, good things will start to happen. For one thing, you'll find your confidence growing. For another, you'll find it easier to create the outcomes that get you closer to where you want to go in life.

I realize that this is a different approach to goal-setting than most people are used to, but I'm okay with that, because most people take an approach to goal-setting that really doesn't work very well. That's because trying to influence things that are on the right side of that "control list" you wrote is as frustrating as trying to capture the wind.

ETHICS

Ethics is your willingness to
act in accordance with clear,
consistent principles that connect
to a sense of right and wrong.

TRANSFORMATIONAL TOPICS:

- ☐ The Principle of the Thing
- ☐ Confident Humility
- ☐ The OK Test
- ☐ You Don't Know!

The Principle of the Thing
Effective leaders
are principled people.

The Principle
of the Thing

An effective leader is a principled person. What does that mean? It means that, in any given situation, you may not be able to predict exactly what the leader's going to do next, but you will always know the principles from which that leader will operate.

How do you know that? Because the leader has made it clear

what his or her convictions and deepest beliefs are.

In our leadership training programs, one of the very first gifts we give those who attend is a blank journal. We encourage participants to label pages with these words:

- Success
- Money
- Your company
- Your market
- Help
- Learning
- Wealthy people
- Poor people

The list goes on. Over the course of the training, they write on those pages what their current set of beliefs are about each of those topics. What have they grown to be convinced of within the realm of that topic? What does the word "success" mean to you? What do you believe about success? What does the word "money" mean to you? What do you believe about money? And so on.

Two interesting things occur as a result of this exercise. One is that people tend to grow their convictions, so that they are in a better position to tell others "This is where I stand — these are my principles." By getting clearer on what each of these topics mean and what the associated beliefs are, people become increasingly principled leaders.

The second interesting result that occurs is that some people uncover previously hidden self-limiting beliefs. It might be a belief placed by a well-meaning parent or other significant adult in the individual's childhood (or even well into adulthood). Or the belief might have been placed there by a manager in whom the person put great confidence and trust.

A self-limiting belief is one that doesn't support you. For example, such a belief might have to do with the meaning you associate with wealthy people: "Wealthy people are significantly different from me." Such a belief would surely create a self-limiting paradigm regarding the growth of your own personal wealth!

Potentially, all of these topics have self-limiting beliefs that can be uncovered if you take the time to inventory your current beliefs and convictions. The goal is to grow towards becoming a principled person — a person of character — a person whom others feel good about trusting, because they know the principles on which you have chosen to live your life.

Confident Humility
Humility does not mean
being timid.

Confident Humility

I believe some leaders suffer from career-limiting timidity due to a false definition of the word "humility." Maybe in their childhood, they were told, "Don't toot your own horn." Or: "Don't get too big for your britches." Or: "Don't get a big head."

As a result, they began to think that humility meant being timid. It doesn't.

There is a continuum to consider here. On the far left-hand side of that continuum, you will find people who are not confident (i.e., people who are timid). Then, as you move along the line you'll see people who are familiar with and confident in their strengths.

This latter group are the people who can make a list of their strengths. They can also make a list of their weaknesses. They can tell you: "Here's what I'm strong at." "Here's what I'm weak at." They can give the details of both lists without blushing. Now for the bad news. Sometimes these are people who come off as unattractive. They revel in their strong suits. They tend to strut, which doesn't wear well on anyone.

Follow the line along.

The continuum moves from "Not confident and timid" to "Knowledgeable about my own strengths" to the third phase: "Confident in my strengths and abilities ... and not taking personal credit for them.

That's Confident Humility. That's the situation where I know my strengths, I know my weaknesses, but I don't take credit or blame for those strengths and weaknesses because I know there are many factors that have affected my development, factors over which I had no control or decision. Examples might be my birth country. I could have been born in Somalia, and I wasn't; the time of my birth — I could have been born when people were dying of the bubonic plague; the gene pool into which I was born; the presence or lack of childhood trauma, and so on. All of those were essentially out of my control.

Please don't send me letters or emails about that last paragraph. I am not in any way suggesting that we use our past as an excuse for our current behaviors. Personal responsibility for what we do with the hand we are dealt is foundational for healthy maturation.

So, do I have strengths? Yes. Do I have weaknesses? Yes. Can I, as a leader, express those with confidence? Yes, but it's when I start taking personal credit for them, then my leadership influence begins to erode. I look prideful, I look egotistical, simply because I start taking credit for those things over which I had no control.

My hope is that you, like the best leaders, can find that Confident Humility balance for yourself.

The OK Test
Don't try to get your ego needs met
during interactions with followers.

The OK Test

When a leader interacts with a follower, only one of the two will get his or her ego needs met. Make sure it's the follower!

If the leader enters the exchange in order to get ego needs met, the follower probably won't. The leader might try to impress the follower with how much he or she knows or how much power he or she wields. As a result, the follower will feel "less OK" than the leader ... and the follower's own ego needs might actually increase as a result of the discussion.

Far better for the leader to "check his or her ego at the door" when entering a meeting with a follower, so as to ensure that the follower feels OK.

Great leaders allow themselves to be taught, rescued, and served by their followers. That way, the follower gets his or her own ego needs met ... and will actually look forward to the next encounter.

You Don't Know!
No matter how old you get, you will never know what you don't know.

You Don't Know!

Strong leaders keeps hubris at bay and their willingness to learn at a consistently high level by remembering this fundamental truth of human affairs: **No matter how old we get, we will never know what we don't know.**

This principle held true for Plato and Socrates. It held true for Cervantes and Shakespeare and Queen Elizabeth I. It held true for Newton and Leibniz and Madame Curie. It held true for Einstein and Gandhi and Mother Teresa. Today, it holds true for Stephen

Hawking and A.S. Byatt and Bill Gates. Consider the achievements of all of those remarkable people, and consider that not one of them knew what they didn't know. Once you do that, you will conclude that there is a pretty good chance that this maxim holds true for you and me, too, no matter however wonderful our potential or our achievements as leaders may be.

We will never know everything. We will never even know what we don't know. This simple conviction acts as a governor on any temptation to pontificate or issue edicts or run ego trips. Remember, a balanced humility permeates the life of a truly great leader.

Expertise is the practical, specific wisdom that causes others to say, "Wow! I didn't see it that way."

TRANSFORMATIONAL TOPICS:

- ☐ Effective Delegation
- ☐ Up-Front Contracts
- ☐ The Pareto Principle
- ☐ Eliminate and Concentrate
- ☐ Your Hourly Wage
- ☐ The Velvet-Covered Brick
- ☐ Epilogue: A Leader's Heart

Effective Delegation
Delegate authority,
not just tasks.

Effective Delegation

Excellent and effective delegation is always a delegation of authority, not merely a delegation of tasks. Many people think of delegation like this: "Here's a list of things I want you to do. In fact, this is how I want you to do it. Check back with me when you're done."

Delegating tasks create followers. Delegating authority creates leaders. Great leaders want to create leaders.

What does it mean to delegate authority? When I delegate

authority, I give the person to whom I'm delegating a "forward" look–saying something like, "Here's what I need done."

I work hard not to go into the "how." I stick to "Here's what I need done," and I'm very explicit about the end result that I want to see. Then I explain the boundaries of the authority I'm delegating. "You can do this to get there, but if you happen to have to do this (cross this line) you need to check with me. You need to check with me before you step over that line."

When I delegate tasks, people will often come back to me and say, "Well now, what shall I do? Shall I do this — or should I do this?"

If I tell them what to do at that time, I've taken all the accountability away from them. If it doesn't work out, they come back and blame me. I'm not building them up as leaders by engaging in that method of delegation.

Instead, I'd say, "You have the authority to make decisions within so-and-so framework. The goal is this — go for it. You can do it."

When you're in a position where you are receiving delegation (i.e., being delegated to), make sure you don't allow your manager to delegate only tasks to you. Help him or her clarify for you the parameters of your authority in carrying out those tasks.

Make sure that you get that from the person who is delegating to you, and make sure that you give that if you happen to be the delegator.

When you give authority, not just tasks, you'll create a culture of great leadership — and not a culture of following.

Up-Front Contracts
Align expectations
ahead of time.

Up-Front Contracts

Once upon a time, two people came to a fork in the road. They decided to sit down and create an up-front agreement about the next leg of their journey.

Now you finish the story!

Some items to which they will need to agree on might involve:

- What's the destination?
- Are they willing to travel the same road together?

- Which direction at the fork will they take?
- Which one of them will take the lead?
- How fast will they proceed?
- At what interval will they evaluate the wisdom of their decision?

Making those decisions prior to beginning the journey will align expectations and cause less tension and misunderstanding in the long run.

Most joint ventures (meetings, sales processes, projects involving two or more people, you name it) will benefit significantly from establishing Up-Front Contracts before proceeding.

Both parties must be willing to "sign the agreement" if there really is to be a shared commitment. If there isn't, both sides should know that.

A well-constructed up-front contract always has five elements:

- The specific objective of the interaction.
- The amount of time required.
- The roles of the participants.
- The actions to be undertaken by the participants.
- The intended outcome of the discussion.

As with anything new, there will be some discomfort the first time you practice an up-front contract. However, the best leaders know this "learning curve" is well worth the investment of time and energy.

The Pareto Principle
Understand and use
the 80-20 rule.

The Pareto Principle

There are many different ways that this oft-cited principle, named after Italian economist Vilfredo Pareto, has been defined and applied.

Sometimes it's referred to as the "80-20 Rule" — 20% of our customers account for 80% of our sales.

Experience has proven this to be true.

Other interpretations include: 80% of the profit is achieved with 20% of the customers, but not necessarily the same 20% as the customers who deliver 80% of the sales. You may have to read that a couple of times, but it will be worthwhile.

Or: 20% of the marketing yields 80% of your campaign's results.

Or: 80% of customer complaints are about the same 20% of your services.

Or: 20% of your time accounts for 80% of your productivity.

Remarkably, all of these are viable conclusions, but since this is a book about leadership, I want to focus on the one regarding time management.

Look at it again: **20% of your time accounts for 80% of your productivity.** Thus, a key component in time management (or energy allocation) is figuring out what 20% of your time is accounting for 80% of your productivity!

For me, this means knowing when to pick my battles. Sometimes, I'm going to be putting in more time than I should, in order to close the gap on some theoretical level of perfection that won't positively affect me or the people in my world.

That time might be more productively used in other pursuits – perhaps in my workplace, perhaps with my family, perhaps engaging exercise. Pick your battles! Make your investments of time and attention consciously! Think about all the different places you could apply "The Pareto Principle" in your own life.

EXPERTISE

Eliminate and Concentrate
Be as good at ending things as
you are at starting things.

Eliminate and Concentrate

Great leaders are not "responsibility hoarders." They seldom take on a new responsibility without eliminating a responsibility they currently have. They are as good at ending things as they are at starting things.

One day, my wife reminded me of this in eloquent terms when she said, "When you don't say 'no' to someone, you are saying 'no' to someone." She meant that when I didn't say "no" to someone who was asking me for a time commitment, I was saying "no" to her! Fair point.

There was a time when I could have taken you to my office and you would have seen a four drawer file cabinet. Three of the drawers were filled with ideas and projects that didn't work out. One drawer was filled with the ideas from which I was making my living at the time.

Mentally that's still how it works. What's in your "hot file"? What might you need to eliminate today so you can concentrate on the truly important priorities in your life?

Your Hourly Wage

Whether he or she is paid by the hour or not, the wise leader knows what the hourly wage is. You can figure this out, too, by taking the amount of money you make and dividing that dollar amount by the number of hours you work. Identify this figure!

This number becomes a guide for removing "clutter" from both your job and other portions of your life.

As a reliable rule of thumb, if someone else will do the job at less than the leader's own hourly wage, then that person should be hired to do the job. In other words, your time may not be utilized to the fullest if large chunks of it are being spent lawn mowing, errand running, bookkeeping, etc.

The possible exception would be anything that brings the leader personal pleasure. Some leaders do enjoy mowing their own lawn.

However, therein lies a dilemma. It is always what the leader likes to do most that is the most difficult to delegate to another. The wise leader is aware of that temptation to hold onto enjoyable but unproductive activities, and avoid from falling prey to that tendency.

The Velvet-Covered Brick
Be easy to approach and nurturing,
but tough when pushed against.

The Velvet-Covered Brick

My hope is that you've not only enjoyed this book, but also have been reminded of some of the key concepts essential to effective leadership. I've always thought of a great leader as being a little like a velvet-covered brick: easy to approach, soft to the touch, nurturing in their leadership style — but tough when pushed against.

People can immediately feel substance in the effective leader. My executive coaching focuses on balancing the velvet-to-brick ratio in each of my mentees. Some are too velvet and need more brick. Some are too "bricky" and need more velvet.

When the right balance is struck between velvet and brick, the strongest leaders emerge. Be such a leader!

Epilogue: A Leader's Heart
Take chances. Strive valiantly. If you fail, at least fail while daring greatly.

Epilogue:
A Leader's Heart

For the conclusion of this book, I offer the words of Theodore Roosevelt, who offered the ultimate observation on leadership when he said:

"It is not the critic who counts, not the man who points out how the strong man stumbles or where the doer of deeds could have done better. The credit belongs to the man who is actually in the arena, whose face is marred by dust and sweat and blood, who strives valiantly, who errs and comes up short again and again, because there is no effort without error or shortcoming, but who knows the great enthusiasms, the great devotions, who spends himself for a worthy cause; who, at the best, knows in the end, the triumph of high achievement, and who, at the worst, if he fails, at least he fails while daring greatly, so that his place shall never be with those cold and timid souls who knew neither victory nor defeat."

May you become the leader reflected in these words.

CONGRATULATIONS!

Transforming Leaders
The Sandler Way
includes a complimentary seminar!

Take this opportunity to personally experience the non-traditional sales training and reinforcement coaching that has been recognized internationally for decades.

Companies in the Fortune 1000 as well as thousands of small-to medium-sized businesses choose Sandler Training for sales, leadership, management, and a wealth of other skill-building programs. Now, it's your turn, and it's free!

You'll learn the latest practical, tactical, feet-in-the-street sales methods directly from your neighborhood Sandler trainers! They're knowledgeable, friendly, and informed about your local selling environment.

Here's how you redeem YOUR FREE SEMINAR invitation.

1. Go to www.Sandler.com and click on the LOCATE A TRAINING CENTER button (upper right corner).
2. Select your location from the drop-down menus.
3. Review the list of all the Sandler trainers in your area.
4. Call your local Sandler trainer, mention *Transforming Leaders The Sandler Way,* and reserve your place at the next seminar!